KATE HALE

Behavioral Issues and Solutions

Effective Ways to Handle Common Challenges

Copyright © 2024 by KATE HALE

All rights reserved. No part of this publication may be reproduced, stored or transmitted in any form or by any means, electronic, mechanical, photocopying, recording, scanning, or otherwise without written permission from the publisher. It is illegal to copy this book, post it to a website, or distribute it by any other means without permission.

First edition

This book was professionally typeset on Reedsy.
Find out more at reedsy.com

Contents

Introduction	1
Understanding Behavioral Development	15
Tantrums, Meltdowns, and Defiance	20
Aggression and Anxiety	32
Attention-Seeking and Social Challenges	44
Positive Reinforcement Techniques	54
Time-Outs and Emotional Regulation	60
Communication and Conflict Resolution	70
Handling ADHD and Autism	84
Addressing Trauma-Related Behaviors	96
Sibling Rivalry and School Conflicts	106
Building Emotional Intelligence	115
Creating a Positive Home Environment	121
Conclusion	127

Introduction

Understanding behavioral challenges in children is a critical aspect of parenting, education, and care giving. From early childhood through adolescence, children exhibit a wide range of behaviors, many of which are considered typical for their developmental stage. However, it's important to recognize when a behavior deviates from the norm and becomes a potential issue that requires intervention. Behavioral challenges may arise due to a combination of genetic, environmental, social, and psychological factors, making it essential to approach them with an informed and compassionate perspective.

Behavioral challenges in children can manifest in various ways, including aggression, defiance, tantrums, anxiety, and social withdrawal. These behaviors often stem from underlying emotions that the child may not know how to express in a healthy way. Factors such as family dynamics, school environment, peer relationships, and even diet and sleep can influence a child's behavior. It is crucial to understand that children are not intentionally trying to be difficult; they are often communicating a need, emotion, or frustration that they don't yet have the skills to verbalize or manage.

One of the key reasons behavioral challenges become problematic is the lack of early intervention. Early intervention matters because it can prevent small issues from escalating into significant behavioral problems later in life. Research has shown that addressing behavioral challenges in early childhood significantly improves the long-term well-being of the child. For example, children who receive appropriate intervention for aggressive behavior or social anxiety are less likely to develop more severe mental health issues, such as depression or conduct disorders, as they grow older.

Early intervention also provides an opportunity to teach children critical coping mechanisms and emotional regulation skills. When behavioral issues are left unaddressed, children may resort to maladaptive coping strategies, such as avoidance, withdrawal, or further acting out. By addressing the root causes of their behavior early on, parents and caregivers can help children develop healthier ways of managing their emotions and interactions with others.

Parents, teachers, and caregivers often ask themselves when it's necessary to seek professional help for a child's behavior. While some challenging behaviors may resolve on their own as the child matures, persistent or escalating behavior problems typically require a structured intervention. Recognizing the signs that a child's behavior has moved beyond typical developmental challenges is key. Signs such as frequent and intense tantrums, aggressive outbursts, difficulty in socializing, or anxiety that interferes with daily functioning are indicators that the child may benefit from professional evaluation and support.

In addition to seeking professional help, parents and caregivers must also understand their pivotal role in managing and addressing behavioral issues. Children model their behaviors and responses from the adults around them. A parent or teacher's reaction to challenging behavior can either reinforce negative behaviors or help the child learn more appropriate ways of responding to stress, frustration, or conflict.

The role of early intervention is not just to correct problematic behaviors but to help children understand themselves better. When children are taught to recognize their emotions and are given the tools to manage them, they develop stronger emotional intelligence, which can lead to more positive outcomes

INTRODUCTION

throughout their lives. Behavioral challenges are often opportunities for growth, both for the child and the caregiver.

As you use this book, remember that each child is unique, and what works for one may not work for another. The strategies and solutions outlined in the following chapters are based on widely accepted practices in child psychology, education, and behavioral intervention. The goal is to provide you with practical tools to better understand and respond to the behaviors you encounter in your daily interactions with children. Keep in mind that patience, consistency, and empathy are key to helping children overcome their behavioral challenges and thrive.

In the following chapters, we will explore the most common behavioral challenges children face and provide effective solutions for addressing them. You will find strategies that range from immediate techniques to manage acute situations, such as tantrums and meltdowns, to long-term approaches for fostering emotional intelligence and resilience. By the end of this book, you will have a comprehensive understanding of how to approach behavioral issues in a way that benefits both the child and the adult.

Understanding Behavioral Development

Children go through various stages of behavioral development, each marked by distinct characteristics and challenges. During these stages, certain behaviors are expected, while others may be cause for concern. Recognizing what is typical for each developmental phase can help parents and caregivers distinguish between normal behavior and potential problems.

In early childhood (ages 1-3), children are learning to navigate their environment and express their desires, often leading to behaviors such as tantrums and defiance. At this stage, children are testing boundaries and exploring their independence, which can result in frustration when they are unable to achieve their goals. While it is normal for toddlers to throw tantrums, excessive or prolonged episodes of anger may indicate difficulty with emotional regulation.

As children enter preschool and early school age (ages 4-7), social interactions become more important, and behavioral issues may arise in response to peer relationships or school expectations. Social anxiety, aggressive behavior, or difficulty following rules may be signs that the child is struggling to adapt to these new demands. At this age, children are also developing their sense of identity and may exhibit oppositional behavior as they assert their independence.

By the time children reach middle childhood (ages 8-12), they have typically developed a broader range of coping skills, but behavioral challenges can still arise, particularly in response to academic pressure or social dynamics. Children in this age group may experience anxiety, defiance, or difficulty with concentration, which can affect their performance at school and their relationships with peers.

Adolescence (ages 13-18) is a time of significant emotional and physical changes, and behavioral challenges are common as teens navigate their growing independence and the social pressures of their environment. Common issues during this stage include defiance, mood swings, anxiety, and risk-taking behaviors. While some degree of rebellion is typical during adolescence, persistent or extreme behaviors may signal underlying emotional or psychological problems.

Understanding these developmental stages and the behaviors that typically accompany them is the first step in addressing behavioral challenges. It is important to view a child's behavior in the context of their developmental stage and recognize that certain behaviors may be appropriate for their age, even if they are challenging for adults to manage. However, when behaviors become disruptive to the child's functioning or are out of proportion to the situation, it may be necessary to intervene.

Tantrums, Meltdowns, and Defiance

Tantrums and meltdowns are among the most common behavioral challenges faced by parents of young children. These emotional outbursts typically occur when a child is frustrated, tired, hungry, or overwhelmed and is unable to express their feelings in a more constructive manner. While tantrums are a normal part of early childhood, frequent or severe episodes may indicate that the child is struggling with emotional regulation.

One of the most effective strategies for managing tantrums is to remain calm and provide the child with a safe space to express their emotions. Yelling or punishing the child during a tantrum can escalate the situation and may reinforce the behavior over time. Instead, parents can help children develop healthier ways of coping with frustration by modeling calm behavior and teaching them to use words to express their needs.

Defiance, or oppositional behavior, is another common challenge, particularly as children seek to assert their independence. While some level of defiance is normal, particularly during the toddler and adolescent years, persistent defiance may indicate an underlying issue, such as oppositional defiant disorder (ODD). Children who exhibit frequent defiance may benefit from structured routines, clear expectations, and consistent consequences for their behavior.

It is also important for parents to understand the triggers that lead to defiant behavior. In many cases, defiance is a reaction to feeling powerless or misunderstood. By offering children choices and involving them in decision-making processes, parents can reduce the likelihood of oppositional behavior.

Aggression and Anxiety

Aggressive behavior in children can be particularly concerning for parents and caregivers. While occasional aggression is normal, especially in response to frustration or conflict, frequent or severe aggressive outbursts may require intervention. Aggression can take many forms, including physical violence, verbal threats, or destructive behavior. It is important to address aggressive behavior early to prevent it from becoming a pattern.

One strategy for addressing aggression is to help the child understand the emotions that lead to aggressive behavior. Often, children become aggressive when they feel overwhelmed by anger, fear, or frustration. Teaching children to identify and label their emotions can help them develop more constructive ways of expressing their feelings. Additionally, providing children with appropriate outlets for their energy, such as physical activity or creative play, can reduce the likelihood of aggressive behavior.

Anxiety is another common behavioral challenge, particularly as children navigate new experiences and social interactions. While some level of anxiety is normal, persistent or overwhelming anxiety can interfere with a child's ability to function. Anxiety may manifest as avoidance, withdrawal, or physical symptoms, such as headaches or stomachaches.

Helping children manage anxiety requires a combination of reassurance, exposure to anxiety-inducing situations, and the development of coping skills. Parents can support anxious children by creating a predictable and supportive environment, offering praise for small successes, and gradually exposing the child to the situations that cause anxiety.

Positive Reinforcement Techniques

INTRODUCTION

Positive reinforcement is one of the most effective tools for shaping behavior in children. Rather than focusing on punishing undesirable behavior, positive reinforcement encourages children to repeat desirable behaviors by offering praise, rewards, or privileges. For example, a child who completes their homework without being reminded might earn extra screen time or a special treat.

To be effective, positive reinforcement must be consistent and specific. General praise, such as "good job," is less effective than specific praise that highlights the behavior, such as "I'm proud of you for sharing with your sister." It is also important to reinforce behaviors immediately after they occur so that the child associates the behavior with the reward.

Parents can use positive reinforcement in conjunction with other strategies, such as setting clear expectations and providing consistent consequences for negative behavior. By focusing on what the child is doing well, rather than what they are doing wrong, parents can create a more positive and cooperative dynamic within the household. This approach not only strengthens the child's confidence and sense of accomplishment but also helps foster a more harmonious and positive environment overall. Positive reinforcement is especially useful in shaping behaviors such as completing chores, following directions, and practicing social skills, as it encourages children to focus on their strengths and achievements.

However, it's essential to avoid over-reliance on material rewards or excessive praise, as this can lead to children developing a sense of entitlement or becoming overly dependent on external validation. Parents should aim to balance tangible rewards, like treats or privileges, with intrinsic reinforcement, such as verbal praise and recognition of the effort the child put into their actions. Over time, this approach helps children internalize good behavior and rely less on external rewards.

Time-Outs and Emotional Regulation

Time-outs are a common disciplinary tool used by parents and caregivers to help children calm down and reflect on their behavior. When used correctly, time-outs can be an effective way to prevent situations from escalating and give the child a moment to regain self-control. The goal of a time-out is not to punish the child but to provide them with a break from the environment or situation that triggered their behavior.

To implement time-outs effectively, parents should clearly explain the reason for the time-out and ensure that the child understands what is expected during this period. Time-outs should be brief, typically one minute for each year of the child's age, and take place in a neutral, non-stimulating environment. Once the time-out is over, it's important for parents to calmly discuss the behavior with the child and offer guidance on how to handle similar situations in the future.

Time-outs can be particularly helpful in managing behaviors such as tantrums, aggression, and defiance, as they provide an opportunity for the child to cool down and reset. However, they should be used in moderation and as part of a broader strategy that includes positive reinforcement and emotional coaching.

In addition to time-outs, helping children develop emotional regulation skills is key to managing behavioral challenges. Emotional regulation refers to the ability to understand and manage emotions in a healthy way. For many children, behavioral issues arise because they lack the skills to cope with strong emotions like anger, frustration, or sadness. By teaching children how to identify and express their emotions appropriately, parents can reduce the likelihood of emotional outbursts and improve the child's overall well-being.

Parents can help children develop emotional regulation by modeling calm behavior, using emotion-focused language, and teaching specific coping strategies, such as deep breathing, counting to ten, or using words to express feelings. Over time, these techniques become valuable tools that children can use to manage their emotions in various situations.

Communication and Conflict Resolution

Effective communication is at the heart of addressing behavioral challenges. When parents and caregivers model clear, respectful communication, children are more likely to learn and adopt these skills in their interactions with others. Children who struggle with behavioral issues often have difficulty expressing their needs, emotions, or frustrations, leading to conflict, defiance, or emotional outbursts. Teaching children how to communicate effectively can reduce these challenges and improve their relationships with both peers and adults.

One key aspect of effective communication is active listening. Parents should make an effort to listen to their child's concerns, frustrations, or feelings without immediately reacting or offering solutions. By acknowledging the child's emotions and showing empathy, parents can create an environment where the child feels heard and understood. This, in turn, makes it easier for the child to express their feelings calmly and constructively.

Teaching children problem-solving and conflict resolution skills is also essential. Conflict is a normal part of social interactions, but children need to learn how to resolve disagreements in a healthy way. Parents can guide children through the process of identifying the problem, considering multiple solutions, and choosing a course of action that takes both their needs and the needs of others into account. This helps children develop critical thinking skills and promotes cooperation and compromise.

When conflicts arise, it's important for parents to stay calm and model appropriate conflict resolution techniques. This may include taking turns to speak, expressing emotions without blaming or accusing, and finding solutions that are fair to everyone involved. Over time, children will learn to apply these skills in their own interactions, leading to fewer conflicts and better outcomes.

Handling ADHD and Autism

Behavioral challenges are often more pronounced in children with specific developmental or neurological conditions, such as Attention Deficit Hyperactivity Disorder (ADHD) or Autism Spectrum Disorder (ASD). These conditions can affect a child's ability to regulate their behavior, focus on tasks, or engage in social interactions, making it especially important for parents and caregivers to understand how to support these children effectively.

Children with ADHD may struggle with impulsivity, hyperactivity, and inattention, which can lead to disruptive behavior in both home and school settings. Managing ADHD-related behavior requires a combination of strategies, including clear structure, consistent routines, and positive reinforcement for good behavior. Break tasks into smaller, manageable steps, and provide frequent breaks to help children with ADHD stay focused and engaged.

It is also important for parents to work closely with teachers and healthcare professionals to develop an individualized behavior plan that addresses the child's specific needs. Medication and behavioral therapy are often recommended for children with ADHD, but these should be discussed with a healthcare provider to determine the best course of action.

Children with ASD may experience difficulties with social communication, sensory sensitivities, and repetitive behaviors. These challenges can lead to frustration, anxiety, or meltdowns, particularly in situations that are unpredictable or overstimulating. Parents of children with ASD can support their child by creating a structured, predictable environment and helping the child learn coping strategies for managing sensory overload or social anxiety.

Visual supports, such as picture schedules or social stories, can be helpful tools for children with ASD, as they provide clear expectations and reduce the uncertainty that often triggers anxiety. Additionally, teaching social skills through role-playing or guided practice can help children with ASD improve their interactions with others.

Addressing Trauma-Related Behaviors

Trauma can have a profound impact on a child's behavior, often leading to emotional dysregulation, anxiety, aggression, or withdrawal. Children who have experienced trauma, such as abuse, neglect, or the loss of a loved one, may exhibit behaviors that are difficult for parents and caregivers to understand or manage. It is important to approach these children with empathy and recognize that their behaviors are often a response to the pain or fear they are carrying.

Trauma-informed care focuses on creating a safe, supportive environment where children feel understood and validated. Parents can help trauma-affected children by offering consistent routines, maintaining clear and predictable boundaries, and providing reassurance during times of stress or uncertainty. It is also important to listen to the child and validate their emotions, even if the behavior itself is challenging.

Therapeutic interventions, such as play therapy or cognitive-behavioral therapy (CBT), are often beneficial for children who have experienced trauma. These therapies help children process their emotions, build coping skills, and develop healthier ways of expressing their feelings. Parents may also benefit from working with a therapist to better understand their child's behavior and learn strategies for supporting their emotional healing.

Sibling Rivalry and School Conflicts

Sibling rivalry is a common behavioral challenge that can create tension and conflict within the household. While some level of competition between siblings is normal, frequent or intense rivalry can lead to negative behaviors, such as jealousy, aggression, or defiance. Addressing sibling rivalry requires a combination of proactive strategies and conflict resolution techniques.

Parents can reduce sibling rivalry by encouraging cooperation and celebrating each child's individual strengths and accomplishments. It's important to avoid comparing siblings or showing favoritism, as this can fuel feelings of resentment or competition. Instead, focus on creating opportunities for siblings to work together on shared tasks or activities, reinforcing positive interactions.

When conflicts between siblings do arise, parents should intervene calmly and fairly, helping the children learn to resolve their disagreements peacefully. Encourage each child to express their feelings and work together to find a solution that respects both perspectives.

School conflicts, whether with peers or teachers, are another common source of behavioral challenges. Children may experience bullying, social exclusion, or academic pressure, all of which can contribute to anxiety, defiance, or aggression. Parents can support their child by maintaining open communication with teachers and school staff, addressing concerns early, and advocating for their child's needs.

INTRODUCTION

It is also important to teach children how to advocate for themselves in school settings. This includes developing communication skills, such as speaking up respectfully when they are being mistreated or struggling with a particular subject. By empowering children to take an active role in resolving school conflicts, parents help build their confidence and self-efficacy.

Building Emotional Intelligence

Emotional intelligence, or the ability to recognize and manage emotions, is a key factor in a child's long-term behavioral and emotional well-being. Children who develop strong emotional intelligence are better equipped to handle stress, resolve conflicts, and build healthy relationships.

Teaching emotional intelligence starts with helping children identify their emotions. This can be done through simple activities, such as labeling emotions in daily situations or using emotion charts. As children become more aware of their feelings, parents can guide them in finding appropriate ways to express and manage those emotions.

Developing empathy is another important aspect of emotional intelligence. Parents can encourage empathy by modeling compassionate behavior, discussing how others might feel in various situations, and encouraging children to consider the perspective of others. Activities such as reading books or watching films that explore different emotions and experiences can also help children build empathy.

Over time, children with strong emotional intelligence are more likely to exhibit positive behaviors, such as cooperation, patience, and problem-solving, while avoiding negative behaviors like aggression or defiance.

By implementing these strategies and solutions, parents and caregivers can effectively address the behavioral challenges their children face. Fostering emotional intelligence, promoting healthy communication, and providing consistent structure and support will set children up for success in managing their behavior, building strong relationships, and navigating the complexities of childhood and adolescence.

Understanding Behavioral Development

Understanding behavioral development is essential for recognizing and addressing common behavioral issues in children. Behavior is influenced by a combination of biological, psychological, social, and environmental factors, and it evolves as children grow. From birth through adolescence, children undergo various developmental stages that shape their behavior, each presenting unique challenges and milestones. By understanding these stages and the underlying influences on behavior, parents, educators, and caregivers can better support children's emotional, cognitive, and social development.

In the earliest years of life, children's behavior is largely driven by their immediate needs and basic survival instincts. Infants communicate primarily through crying, cooing, and body language, as they lack the verbal and emotional skills to express their needs more directly. This stage, typically lasting from birth to around 18 months, is characterized by attachment behaviors. Infants rely heavily on their caregivers for safety, food, and comfort, and they form strong emotional bonds during this time. The quality of these early relationships is critical, as it lays the foundation for future emotional regulation and social interactions.

As children grow into toddlers, typically between the ages of one and three, their behavior becomes more exploratory and independent. During this period, children begin to assert their autonomy and test boundaries, which often manifests in behaviors such as tantrums, defiance, and curiosity-driven actions. This is a time of rapid brain development, particularly in areas related to language, motor skills, and emotional regulation. While some of the challenging behaviors at this stage, such as frustration and impatience, may seem difficult to manage, they are a normal part of a child's development as they learn to navigate the world around them.

One of the key developmental milestones during the toddler years is the onset of language acquisition. As children learn to speak, their ability to express their needs and emotions expands. This, in turn, can reduce some of the frustration that leads to negative behaviors. However, because toddlers are still learning to regulate their emotions and communicate effectively, they may become overwhelmed when they cannot get their way or when they experience a lack of control over their environment. It's important for caregivers to recognize that many behavioral issues during this stage stem from a child's limited ability to communicate and self-soothe.

By the time children reach preschool age, around three to five years old, they begin to engage in more complex social interactions with peers. This is a critical period for social and emotional development, as children start to develop friendships, share, and engage in cooperative play. However, it is also a time when children may exhibit possessiveness, jealousy, or aggression as they learn to navigate social dynamics. Behaviors such as hitting, pushing, or refusal to share are common, but they can be addressed by teaching children appropriate ways to express their emotions and resolve conflicts.

As children enter early school age, typically between five and seven years old, their behavior continues to be shaped by their expanding cognitive abilities and social experiences. During this stage, children begin to understand the concept of rules and consequences, which can lead to both positive and negative behaviors. For example, children may exhibit increased compliance with authority figures, such as parents and teachers, but they may also become more aware of their ability to challenge rules or seek attention through disruptive behavior. Peer relationships become increasingly important, and children may face new challenges, such as exclusion, bullying, or the pressure to conform to group norms.

In this stage, children are developing a stronger sense of self and identity, which can lead to behaviors that reflect their desire for autonomy and independence. They may test limits, argue, or display defiant behaviors as they assert their individuality. It's important for parents and caregivers to provide consistent boundaries while also encouraging the child's growing independence. Positive reinforcement, praise, and constructive discipline techniques are essential in helping children learn appropriate behavior while fostering their self-confidence.

The next major stage of behavioral development occurs during middle childhood, from approximately seven to twelve years old. At this age, children are refining their social skills and learning to navigate more complex interpersonal relationships. School plays a central role in their lives, and academic performance, peer relationships, and extracurricular activities all contribute to their behavioral development. Children may face pressures related to academic achievement, friendships, and fitting in, which can lead to behaviors such as anxiety, defiance, or withdrawal if they struggle to cope with these demands.

Middle childhood is also a time when children become more aware of societal expectations and their place within various social groups. Peer acceptance becomes increasingly important, and children may begin to modify their behavior to align with peer group norms. This can sometimes result in positive behaviors, such as increased cooperation and empathy, but it can also lead to negative behaviors, such as peer pressure or bullying. It's important for parents and caregivers to maintain open communication with children during this stage, helping them navigate social challenges and teaching them how to assert themselves in healthy ways.

By the time children reach adolescence, from around twelve to eighteen years old, behavioral development takes on new dimensions. Adolescence is a period of significant physical, emotional, and psychological change, driven by hormonal shifts, brain development, and the transition from childhood to adulthood. Teenagers begin to form their own identities, explore independence, and seek more control over their lives. This can lead to behaviors such as risk-taking, defiance, and mood swings, as adolescents grapple with the challenges of growing up.

During adolescence, peer influence is particularly strong, and teens may engage in behaviors aimed at gaining social approval or asserting their individuality. Experimentation with boundaries, whether through testing authority, engaging in risky behaviors, or exploring new social roles, is common. While some of this behavior is part of normal adolescent development, it can also lead to problematic actions if not properly guided. For example, risky behaviors such as substance use, truancy, or dangerous driving can have serious consequences if left unchecked.

Adolescents also face increased emotional volatility due to the combination of hormonal changes and the cognitive and social pressures of this stage of life. They may experience intense emotions, such as anger, sadness, or anxiety, which can lead to behaviors like rebellion, withdrawal, or confrontation with authority figures. Understanding the emotional challenges that adolescents face is key to supporting them through this turbulent time and helping them develop healthier coping strategies.

In addition to the emotional and social challenges of adolescence, cognitive development plays a major role in shaping behavior. Adolescents are developing more advanced reasoning and problem-solving skills, and they begin to think more abstractly and critically about the world around them. This cognitive growth allows them to question authority, challenge societal norms, and develop their own moral and ethical beliefs. While this is an important part of becoming an independent adult, it can also lead to conflicts with parents and other authority figures, as teens seek to assert their own values and make decisions independently.

Throughout all these stages of development, it's important to recognize that behavior is influenced by a range of factors, including genetics, temperament, and environmental influences. While some children may be naturally more compliant, others may be more prone to defiance or emotional outbursts. Similarly, a child's behavior can be shaped by family dynamics, cultural norms, and the specific challenges they face at home, school, or in their community. It's also important to remember that while certain behaviors may be typical for a particular developmental stage, every child is unique and may experience these stages at their own pace.

Parents, educators, and caregivers play a critical role in supporting children through each stage of behavioral development. Consistent and positive parenting, clear boundaries, and open communication are essential for helping children develop the skills they need to navigate challenges and regulate their behavior. By providing a supportive environment that fosters emotional resilience, social competence, and self-regulation, adults can help children thrive and grow into well-adjusted individuals.

Ultimately, understanding behavioral development involves recognizing the complex interplay between a child's biological, emotional, and social growth. It also requires patience, empathy, and a commitment to guiding children through their behavioral challenges with compassion and consistency. By taking a proactive approach to understanding and addressing behavioral issues, parents and caregivers can lay the groundwork for healthy development and positive behaviors throughout childhood and adolescence.

Tantrums, Meltdowns, and Defiance

Tantrums, meltdowns, and defiance are among the most common and challenging behaviors parents and caregivers face when raising children. These behaviors often occur during early childhood, but they can persist into later stages if not properly addressed. Understanding why these behaviors happen and how to manage them effectively is crucial for fostering emotional regulation, healthy communication, and overall behavioral development in children.

Tantrums are emotional outbursts characterized by crying, yelling, stomping, or even physical aggression like hitting or kicking. They are most common in toddlers and preschoolers, typically starting between the ages of 1 and 3, when children are beginning to assert their independence but have limited verbal skills and emotional regulation. Tantrums can occur in response to frustration, exhaustion, hunger, or unmet desires. While they are a normal part of development, frequent or severe tantrums can be disruptive and stressful for both the child and the adult involved.

Meltdowns, while similar to tantrums, are often more intense and prolonged. They usually occur when a child becomes overwhelmed by sensory stimuli, strong emotions, or an inability to process their environment. Meltdowns can be particularly common in children with sensory processing issues or neurodevelopmental conditions like autism spectrum disorder (ASD). Unlike tantrums, which can sometimes be attention-seeking or goal-oriented (for example, to get a toy or a treat), meltdowns are more about the child losing control over their emotions or becoming overstimulated.

Defiance, on the other hand, is when children actively refuse to follow instructions or comply with requests from adults. This can range from simply saying "no" to throwing objects, refusing to move, or deliberately doing the opposite of what is asked. Defiant behavior often begins during the toddler years, as children start testing boundaries and asserting their autonomy. However, defiance can persist into later childhood and adolescence, especially if not handled constructively. While some level of defiance is a normal part of growing up, consistent or extreme defiant behavior can be indicative of deeper issues, such as Oppositional Defiant Disorder (ODD).

In understanding the underlying causes of tantrums, meltdowns, and defiance, it's important to recognize that young children are still developing the emotional and cognitive skills needed to regulate their behavior. They are learning to navigate a complex world where they do not always get what they want, where boundaries are enforced, and where their emotions often feel overwhelming. As a result, behaviors like tantrums and defiance are expressions of these struggles. By teaching children how to manage their emotions and providing them with tools to navigate these challenges, adults can help reduce the frequency and intensity of these behaviors.

Tantrums: Causes and Management Strategies

Tantrums often occur because young children have not yet developed the language or emotional regulation skills to handle frustration or disappointment. When a child wants something and is told "no," or when they feel hungry, tired, or overstimulated, they may experience a flood of emotions that they don't know how to process. This leads to the classic tantrum response: crying, yelling, and, in some cases, physical aggression.

One key strategy for managing tantrums is to recognize and address the child's basic needs before they reach the point of emotional overwhelm.

Ensuring that the child is well-rested, fed, and not overstimulated can help prevent tantrums from occurring. In addition, setting clear expectations and providing consistent routines can give children a sense of control and security, reducing the likelihood of frustration-induced tantrums.

When a tantrum does occur, it's important for the adult to remain calm and avoid escalating the situation. Yelling at or punishing the child during a tantrum can often make the behavior worse, as the child is already overwhelmed and may not have the capacity to respond rationally. Instead, caregivers should acknowledge the child's feelings by saying something like, "I can see you're very upset right now," while offering comfort and support.

In some cases, ignoring the tantrum can be an effective strategy, particularly if the behavior is attention-seeking. However, this should be done carefully, as ignoring a child who is genuinely distressed or overwhelmed may make the situation worse. The key is to assess whether the tantrum is a result of frustration and lack of control, or whether it's an attempt to manipulate the situation to get what they want.

It can also be helpful to give the child a safe space to express their emotions. This might mean removing them from a public or overstimulating environment and giving them time to calm down. Once the child has calmed, caregivers should gently explain why the tantrum was not an appropriate response and offer alternative ways to express frustration. For example, teaching children to use their words to express what they want or how they are feeling can help prevent future tantrums.

Over time, children can be taught coping strategies, such as deep breathing, counting to ten, or using a calm-down corner. These techniques give the child a way to manage their emotions before they reach the point of a full-blown tantrum. It's important to reinforce positive behavior by praising the child when they handle frustration appropriately, helping them understand that there are better ways to express their emotions than through tantrums.

Meltdowns: Causes and Management Strategies

Meltdowns are different from tantrums in that they are often less about a child's desire to get something and more about being overwhelmed by sensory input or emotional overload. Children experiencing meltdowns may have difficulty calming themselves down without external help, and the behavior can be more intense and longer-lasting than a typical tantrum.

For children with sensory sensitivities, meltdowns can occur when they are exposed to loud noises, bright lights, crowded spaces, or other sensory stimuli that they find overwhelming. These meltdowns are not intentional and are not about trying to manipulate a situation; rather, they are the result of the child's nervous system becoming overwhelmed.

In managing meltdowns, it's important to recognize the child's triggers and create environments that minimize those triggers. For example, if a child is sensitive to loud noises, offering them noise-canceling headphones or finding quieter spaces can help reduce the likelihood of a meltdown. Similarly, using visual schedules or social stories can help prepare children for transitions or changes in routine, which can often be a trigger for meltdowns in children with autism or other neurodevelopmental conditions.

When a meltdown occurs, caregivers should focus on calming the child rather than trying to reason with them. Meltdowns are not the time for teaching or discipline, as the child is not in a state where they can process information or respond rationally. Instead, offer comfort and reduce sensory input by moving to a quieter space or dimming lights if possible. Physical comfort, such as a gentle hug or sitting quietly with the child, can sometimes help, but it's important to respect the child's boundaries if they do not want physical contact.

After the child has calmed down, it may be helpful to discuss what happened and explore ways to prevent future meltdowns. This conversation should be gentle and focused on understanding the child's feelings, rather than on blame or punishment. Teaching children self-regulation strategies, such as deep breathing, using sensory tools (like fidget toys), or asking for a break when they feel overwhelmed, can empower them to manage their emotions more effectively.

It's also important to note that meltdowns are often more common in children who have difficulty with sensory processing or emotional regulation, such as those with autism, ADHD, or anxiety disorders. In these cases, working with a therapist or specialist to develop a comprehensive behavior plan can be beneficial in addressing the root causes of meltdowns and teaching the child coping skills.

Defiance: Causes and Management Strategies

Defiance is another common behavioral challenge in young children, especially during the toddler and preschool years when children are learning to assert their independence. While some degree of defiance is normal and developmentally appropriate, persistent or extreme defiance can create significant challenges for parents and caregivers.

Defiant behavior often occurs when a child feels powerless or out of control. By saying "no" or refusing to comply with a request, the child is exerting their autonomy and testing the limits of their environment. This behavior is particularly common during the "terrible twos," when children are beginning to develop a sense of self and independence but may not yet have the emotional maturity to navigate complex social dynamics.

One of the most effective ways to manage defiance is to offer children choices whenever possible. Giving children a sense of control over their environment can reduce the need for defiant behavior. For example, instead of telling a child to get dressed, offer them a choice between two outfits. This allows the child to feel empowered while still following the desired behavior. Offering choices can also be effective in situations where the child is resisting bedtime, mealtimes, or other routine activities.

Setting clear, consistent boundaries is also essential in managing defiant behavior. Children need to know what is expected of them and what the consequences will be if they do not comply. It's important to follow through on consequences in a calm and consistent manner, as inconsistency can lead to confusion and further defiance. However, consequences should be reasonable and related to the behavior. For example, if a child refuses to clean up their toys, a logical consequence might be that they lose the privilege of playing with those toys for the rest of the day.

Positive reinforcement is another powerful tool for reducing defiant behavior. Children are more likely to repeat behaviors that are rewarded, so it's important to praise them when they follow instructions or comply with requests. Rather than focusing solely on the defiant behavior, caregivers should highlight the moments when the child is cooperative and compliant. This positive attention reinforces the idea that good behavior leads to positive outcomes.

It's also important to understand the underlying emotions that may be driving defiant behavior. Children who feel frustrated, anxious, or overwhelmed are more likely to act out in defiance. By addressing the root cause of the child's emotions and helping them develop coping strategies, caregivers can reduce the frequency and intensity of defiant behaviors. For instance, if a child is acting out because they are anxious about a new situation, such as starting school, it may help to talk through their feelings and offer reassurance. Identifying the emotional triggers behind defiance allows caregivers to address the child's needs proactively rather than simply reacting to the behavior itself.

Another approach to managing defiance is the use of "time-in" strategies, which differ from the traditional "time-out" method. In a time-in, instead of isolating the child as punishment, the caregiver stays close to the child and helps them work through their emotions in a supportive manner. This approach emphasizes connection and emotional coaching, helping the child understand their feelings and why their behavior is unacceptable. Over time, this strategy can help children develop emotional regulation skills and reduce their reliance on defiance as a means of coping with frustration or powerlessness.

Parents and caregivers should also be mindful of their own behavior when dealing with defiance. Children often mirror the actions and attitudes of the adults around them, so it's important to model calm, respectful communication even in challenging situations. If a child sees an adult responding to conflict with anger or harshness, they are more likely to adopt similar behaviors. On the other hand, modeling patience, problem-solving, and respectful dialogue can teach children how to handle conflict without resorting to defiance.

In cases where defiant behavior is persistent and disruptive, it may be necessary to seek professional help. Some children may develop patterns of defiance that are indicative of deeper behavioral issues, such as Oppositional Defiant Disorder (ODD). ODD is characterized by a pattern of angry, irritable mood, argumentative or defiant behavior, and vindictiveness toward authority figures. Children with ODD often struggle with impulse control and emotional regulation, leading to frequent conflicts at home and school. Early intervention with behavioral therapy and family counseling can be highly effective in helping children with ODD learn more constructive ways to manage their emotions and behavior.

The Role of Consistency and Routine

One of the most effective ways to prevent and manage tantrums, meltdowns, and defiance is by establishing a consistent routine. Children thrive on predictability, and a structured daily routine provides them with a sense of security and control over their environment. When children know what to expect, they are less likely to become frustrated or anxious, reducing the likelihood of emotional outbursts or defiant behavior.

For younger children, having set times for meals, naps, play, and bedtime can create a stable framework that helps them regulate their emotions and energy levels. Predictable routines also allow children to anticipate transitions, which can be a major source of frustration for toddlers and preschoolers. For example, giving a child a five-minute warning before it's time to clean up toys or leave the playground can help them mentally prepare for the change, reducing resistance and tantrums.

In addition to daily routines, setting consistent behavioral expectations is crucial. Children need to understand the boundaries of acceptable behavior and the consequences for crossing those boundaries. Consistency in enforcing rules and consequences helps children internalize expectations and reduces confusion or mixed messages. For example, if a child knows that hitting a sibling always results in a time-out, they are more likely to learn to avoid this behavior over time.

While consistency is important, it's also necessary to be flexible when appropriate. Rigid enforcement of rules without consideration of the child's emotional state can sometimes backfire, leading to more defiance or emotional distress. For example, if a child is overtired or feeling unwell, they may be more prone to meltdowns or defiance, and adjusting expectations in these situations can help de-escalate the behavior. The key is to strike a balance between maintaining consistent expectations and recognizing when a child's behavior is influenced by external factors that require empathy and adjustment.

Teaching Emotional Regulation Skills

A key element in managing tantrums, meltdowns, and defiance is teaching children how to regulate their emotions. Emotional regulation is the ability to recognize, understand, and manage one's emotions in a healthy way, and it is a critical skill for reducing negative behaviors. Children who struggle with emotional regulation are more likely to react to frustration, disappointment, or sensory overload with tantrums, meltdowns, or defiance.

One of the first steps in teaching emotional regulation is helping children identify and label their emotions. Young children often have difficulty understanding what they are feeling, which can lead to emotional outbursts when they become overwhelmed. Caregivers can support emotional literacy by using simple language to describe emotions during everyday interactions. For example, saying, "It looks like you're feeling angry because you can't have the toy right now," helps the child understand their emotions and begin to connect their feelings to their behavior.

Once children are able to identify their emotions, they can begin learning strategies for managing them. Deep breathing exercises, counting to ten, or using calming phrases like "I can handle this" are simple but effective techniques that can help children calm down when they feel frustrated or upset. These strategies can be practiced during calm moments so that children are more likely to use them during emotionally charged situations.

In addition to individual coping strategies, caregivers can model emotional regulation by demonstrating how they handle their own emotions in challenging situations. Children are observant and often mimic the behaviors of adults, so it's important for caregivers to show how they manage stress, frustration, or anger in constructive ways. For example, if a parent is feeling overwhelmed, they might say, "I'm feeling frustrated right now, so I'm going to take a few deep breaths to calm down." This not only models healthy behavior but also reinforces the idea that everyone, including adults, needs to manage their emotions.

Using positive reinforcement to encourage emotional regulation is also important. When a child successfully uses a coping strategy to manage their emotions, it's important to acknowledge and praise their efforts. This reinforces the idea that emotional regulation is a skill to be valued and celebrated, making it more likely that the child will continue to practice these behaviors.

The Importance of Empathy and Connection

Empathy and connection play a crucial role in managing behavioral challenges like tantrums, meltdowns, and defiance. Children who feel understood, valued, and connected to their caregivers are more likely to respond positively to guidance and discipline. On the other hand, children who feel disconnected or misunderstood may become more defiant or emotionally volatile.

Empathy involves seeing the world from the child's perspective and acknowledging their feelings, even if their behavior is difficult. For example, when a child is throwing a tantrum because they can't have a snack before dinner, it's important for the caregiver to validate their frustration: "I know you're upset because you're hungry, but we have to wait until dinner." This approach shows the child that their feelings are heard and respected, even if the behavior itself is not acceptable.

Building strong emotional connections with children also helps reduce defiance and emotional outbursts. Children who feel secure in their relationships with caregivers are more likely to cooperate and follow instructions. Spending quality time together, engaging in play, and offering physical affection are simple but effective ways to strengthen these bonds. When children feel connected to their caregivers, they are more motivated to behave well because they value the relationship.

It's also important to approach discipline from a place of teaching rather than punishment. When children act out, they are often communicating a need or emotion that they don't yet have the skills to express appropriately.

Instead of focusing solely on the negative behavior, caregivers should use these moments as opportunities to teach problem-solving and emotional regulation. For example, if a child is defiant because they don't want to clean up their toys, the caregiver might say, "I understand you don't want to clean up right now, but we need to take care of our things. How about we make it fun and clean up together?"

By using empathy, connection, and teaching moments, caregivers can create a supportive environment where children feel understood and capable of managing their emotions and behavior. Over time, this approach helps children develop the emotional resilience and social skills they need to navigate challenges without resorting to tantrums, meltdowns, or defiance.

Seeking Professional Help

While most tantrums, meltdowns, and defiance are a normal part of childhood development, there are times when these behaviors may be indicative of a deeper issue that requires professional intervention. If a child's behavior is persistently disruptive, extreme, or affecting their ability to function at home, school, or in social situations, it may be time to seek help from a pediatrician, psychologist, or behavioral therapist.

Children with conditions such as ADHD, autism spectrum disorder, anxiety disorders, or mood disorders may experience more frequent or severe behavioral challenges. These children can benefit from targeted interventions, such as behavioral therapy, social skills training, or, in some cases, medication. Early intervention can make a significant difference in helping children develop the skills they need to manage their behavior and succeed in everyday life.

Caregivers should not hesitate to seek support if they feel overwhelmed or unsure of how to manage their child's behavior. Professional guidance can provide valuable insights and strategies for addressing challenging behaviors while supporting the child's emotional and social development.

In conclusion, tantrums, meltdowns, and defiance are common but manageable aspects of childhood. Through consistent routines, emotional regulation strategies, empathy, and strong connections, caregivers can guide children through these challenging behaviors, helping them grow into emotionally resilient and well-adjusted individuals.

Aggression and Anxiety

Aggression and anxiety are two behavioral challenges that, while seemingly distinct, often share common roots in emotional dysregulation, frustration, and environmental triggers. Both behaviors can be distressing for the children experiencing them and for the caregivers, teachers, or peers affected by these outbursts or episodes. Understanding the causes, manifestations, and management strategies for aggression and anxiety is crucial in helping children navigate these intense emotions and preventing long-term behavioral or emotional difficulties.

Aggression in children can manifest in various forms, from verbal outbursts like yelling, insults, or threats, to physical behaviors such as hitting, kicking, biting, or pushing. Aggressive behavior often arises from feelings of frustration, anger, or a perceived lack of control over a situation. Children may become aggressive when they feel their needs are not being met, when they are overwhelmed by external stimuli, or when they are unable to articulate their emotions or desires. In some cases, aggression may be a learned behavior, modeled after the actions of others around them, whether that be parents, siblings, or peers.

Anxiety, on the other hand, is typically characterized by feelings of worry, fear, or unease, often about future events or potential outcomes. Children with anxiety may exhibit behaviors such as withdrawal, avoidance of specific situations, restlessness, irritability, or physical symptoms like stomachaches, headaches, or trembling. While anxiety and aggression may seem to be on opposite ends of the emotional spectrum, they often coexist, with anxious children sometimes lashing out in frustration or fear, leading to aggressive behaviors.

Both aggression and anxiety can be triggered by a wide range of factors, including genetic predispositions, environmental stressors, developmental challenges, and social pressures. Addressing these behaviors requires a comprehensive understanding of their causes and the implementation of strategies that help children develop emotional regulation skills, build resilience, and feel secure in their environment.

Understanding the Causes of Aggression

Aggression in children is not necessarily a sign of inherent defiance or anger; rather, it is often a signal that a child is struggling with underlying emotional or psychological difficulties. Understanding the causes of aggressive behavior can help caregivers and educators address the root issues rather than simply reacting to the behavior itself.

One common cause of aggression is frustration. Young children, especially toddlers and preschoolers, are still developing their language and communication skills. When they are unable to express their needs or feelings effectively, they may become frustrated, leading to aggressive outbursts. For example, a child who wants a toy that another child is playing with may resort to hitting or pushing because they don't yet have the verbal skills to negotiate or ask for a turn. In this case, aggression is not a sign of deliberate meanness but a reflection of the child's developmental stage and their difficulty in managing frustration.

Sensory overload is another frequent trigger for aggressive behavior, particularly in children with sensory processing issues. Children who are hypersensitive to stimuli such as loud noises, bright lights, or crowded environments may become overwhelmed and react aggressively as a way of coping with the discomfort. For these children, the aggression is a defensive mechanism, a way of asserting control over an environment that feels chaotic or threatening.

In some cases, aggression can be learned behavior. Children may observe aggressive actions in others—whether through family members, peers, or even media—and imitate these behaviors. If a child witnesses adults responding to conflict with yelling, hitting, or other forms of aggression, they may come to see these behaviors as acceptable ways to handle frustration or resolve disputes. Similarly, if a child is bullied or exposed to aggressive peers, they may adopt aggressive behaviors as a means of self-protection or to assert dominance in social situations.

Emotional trauma and stress are also significant contributors to aggressive behavior. Children who have experienced trauma, such as abuse, neglect, or witnessing violence, may develop aggressive tendencies as a result of the intense emotions they are carrying. For these children, aggression may be a way of expressing their inner turmoil, fear, or anger, especially if they have not been given the tools to process their emotions in a healthy way.

Lastly, developmental disorders such as Attention Deficit Hyperactivity Disorder (ADHD), Oppositional Defiant Disorder (ODD), and autism spectrum disorder (ASD) are often associated with aggressive behaviors. Children with these conditions may struggle with impulse control, emotional regulation, and social skills, making them more prone to acting out in aggressive ways when they are frustrated or overwhelmed.

Addressing and Managing Aggression

Managing aggressive behavior in children requires a multifaceted approach that addresses both the immediate behavior and the underlying causes. Caregivers and educators must remain calm and consistent when dealing with aggression, providing children with clear boundaries and helping them develop healthier ways of expressing their emotions.

One of the most effective strategies for managing aggression is teaching children emotional regulation skills. Emotional regulation involves the ability to recognize and manage one's emotions, and it is a skill that children need to be taught and practiced over time. When a child becomes aggressive, it is often because they feel overwhelmed by their emotions and don't know how to express them in a constructive way. Caregivers can help by acknowledging the child's feelings and teaching them alternative ways to cope with frustration or anger. For example, a child who is prone to hitting when angry can be taught to use words to express their feelings or to take deep breaths to calm down before reacting.

Providing children with a safe space to express their emotions can also be helpful in reducing aggression. For instance, creating a calm-down corner or a quiet space where the child can retreat when they are feeling overwhelmed can give them the opportunity to regain control of their emotions before the situation escalates into aggression. Over time, children can learn to recognize the signs that they are becoming upset and take proactive steps to calm themselves down before they act out.

Positive reinforcement is another powerful tool in managing aggressive behavior. Children are more likely to repeat behaviors that are rewarded, so it's important to praise them when they handle frustration or conflict in a constructive way. For example, if a child who typically reacts with aggression is able to walk away from a frustrating situation or use words to express their feelings, caregivers should acknowledge and reinforce this positive behavior. Over time, positive reinforcement helps children internalize the idea that there are better ways to handle their emotions than through aggression.

Setting clear and consistent boundaries is also crucial in managing aggressive behavior. Children need to understand what behaviors are acceptable and what the consequences will be if they act aggressively. Consistency in enforcing rules and consequences helps children feel secure and understand that aggressive behavior is not tolerated. However, consequences should be logical and related to the behavior. For example, if a child hits a sibling, a logical consequence might be a time-out to reflect on their actions, followed by a discussion about how to handle frustration in the future.

In cases where aggression is linked to sensory processing issues or developmental disorders, specialized interventions may be necessary. Occupational therapy, sensory integration therapy, or behavioral therapy can help children with sensory sensitivities or developmental delays learn to manage their emotions and reactions more effectively. In some cases, medication may also be recommended, particularly for children with conditions like ADHD or severe anxiety that contribute to aggressive outbursts.

Understanding the Causes of Anxiety

Anxiety in children is a common yet often misunderstood condition. While it is normal for children to experience some level of fear or worry in certain situations—such as starting school, going to the doctor, or encountering new social environments—persistent or intense anxiety can interfere with a child's daily life and overall well-being. Children with anxiety may struggle with fears that are disproportionate to the situation, and their anxiety may manifest in a variety of ways, including avoidance behaviors, physical symptoms, and emotional distress.

One of the most common forms of anxiety in children is separation anxiety, which typically occurs in toddlers and preschoolers but can persist into later childhood if not addressed. Separation anxiety is characterized by excessive fear or worry about being away from a primary caregiver. Children with separation anxiety may cry, cling to their caregiver, or refuse to go to school or other activities where they are separated from their parent. While some level of separation anxiety is normal in young children, extreme or prolonged anxiety can impact the child's social development and academic performance.

Social anxiety is another common form of anxiety in children, particularly as they enter school and begin interacting with peers. Children with social anxiety may be extremely self-conscious, fear judgment or embarrassment, and avoid social situations such as group activities, speaking in front of others, or interacting with new people. Social anxiety can lead to withdrawal, isolation, and difficulty forming friendships, which can further exacerbate the child's anxiety.

Generalized anxiety disorder (GAD) is characterized by excessive and uncontrollable worry about a wide range of everyday situations. Children with GAD may worry about their performance in school, the health and safety of their family, natural disasters, or other unlikely events. This constant worry can lead to physical symptoms such as headaches, stomachaches, and fatigue, as well as emotional symptoms like irritability, restlessness, and difficulty concentrating.

Anxiety in children can also be triggered by traumatic experiences or major life changes. For example, children who have experienced the death of a loved one, divorce, moving to a new home, or a change in caregivers may develop anxiety as they cope with the uncertainty and stress of these events. Additionally, children who have been exposed to chronic stress, such as living in an unsafe environment or experiencing bullying, are more likely to develop anxiety.

In some cases, anxiety may have a genetic component, with children inheriting a predisposition to anxiety from their parents. Children who have a parent with an anxiety disorder are more likely to develop anxiety themselves, as they may both inherit the genetic tendency and learn anxious behaviors from their environment.

Addressing and Managing Anxiety

Managing anxiety in children requires a compassionate and proactive approach that helps them develop coping skills and feel secure in their environment. The goal is not to eliminate anxiety altogether—some level of anxiety is a normal and necessary part of life—but to help children learn how to manage their anxiety in a healthy way so that it doesn't interfere with their daily functioning or overall well-being. Helping children build resilience and confidence in the face of anxiety is key to their long-term emotional health.

One of the first steps in addressing anxiety is teaching children to recognize and name their anxious feelings. Young children may not have the vocabulary to describe what they are experiencing, so caregivers can help by offering simple language to label the emotions. For example, saying, "It seems like you're feeling worried about going to school" helps the child understand that what they are experiencing is anxiety, not something inherently wrong with them. Once children can identify their feelings, they can begin learning how to manage them.

A common technique for managing anxiety is cognitive-behavioral therapy (CBT), which helps children identify and challenge negative thought patterns that contribute to their anxiety. CBT teaches children to recognize when they are engaging in "catastrophic thinking" (imagining the worst-case scenario) and to replace these thoughts with more realistic, balanced perspectives. For instance, a child who is anxious about a test may be taught to replace the thought "I'm going to fail and everyone will think I'm stupid" with "I've studied hard, and even if I don't get a perfect score, I'll still be okay."

Caregivers can reinforce this approach by modeling positive thinking and helping children re-frame their anxious thoughts in everyday situations. For example, if a child is worried about making a mistake during a school presentation, a parent might say, "It's okay to be nervous. Everyone makes mistakes sometimes, but what's important is that you try your best." This helps the child see that mistakes are a normal part of life and not something to be feared.

Exposure therapy is another effective technique for managing anxiety, particularly for children with specific fears or phobias. The idea behind exposure therapy is to gradually and systematically expose the child to the source of their fear in a controlled and supportive environment, helping them build confidence and reduce their anxiety over time. For example, if a child is afraid of dogs, they might start by looking at pictures of dogs, then progress to watching dogs from a distance, and eventually work up to petting a calm, friendly dog. Each step is taken slowly, with the child's comfort level guiding the pace of progress.

Relaxation techniques such as deep breathing, progressive muscle relaxation, and mindfulness exercises can also be highly effective in managing anxiety. Teaching children to use deep breathing during moments of anxiety can help them calm their nervous system and regain control over their emotions. A simple exercise like "belly breathing," where the child breathes in deeply through their nose, holds the breath for a moment, and then slowly exhales through their mouth, can be practiced during calm moments so that the child is prepared to use it during times of stress.

Progressive muscle relaxation involves teaching children to tense and then relax different muscle groups in their body, helping them release physical tension that often accompanies anxiety. Mindfulness exercises, such as focusing on the sensations of breathing or paying attention to the sounds and sights around them, can help anxious children stay grounded in the present moment rather than getting lost in worry about the future.

In some cases, anxiety may be severe enough that professional intervention is necessary. Therapy with a trained counselor or psychologist can provide children with additional tools and support for managing their anxiety. Cognitive-behavioral therapy is one of the most well-researched and effective forms of treatment for childhood anxiety, but other therapeutic approaches, such as play therapy or family counseling, may also be beneficial depending on the child's specific needs.

In certain cases, medication may be recommended to help manage severe anxiety, particularly if it is interfering with the child's ability to function in daily life. Medications such as selective serotonin re-uptake inhibitors (Saris) can help regulate the brain's chemistry and reduce the symptoms of anxiety. However, medication is typically considered a last resort and is usually combined with therapy and behavioral interventions to provide a holistic approach to treatment.

Caregivers play a crucial role in supporting children with anxiety by providing a safe, nurturing environment where the child feels understood and validated. It's important to listen to the child's concerns and offer reassurance without dismissing their feelings. While it's tempting to try to "fix" the problem or provide quick solutions, simply acknowledging the child's anxiety and being present with them in their moment of fear can be incredibly comforting.

At the same time, caregivers must strike a balance between offering support and encouraging independence. Overprotecting an anxious child or allowing them to avoid situations that trigger their anxiety can reinforce the fear and prevent the child from developing coping skills. Instead, caregivers should gently encourage the child to face their fears in small, manageable steps, offering praise and support for each step of progress. This helps the child build confidence and resilience, knowing that they are capable of managing their anxiety.

Routine and structure are also important for children with anxiety, as predictability can help reduce feelings of uncertainty and fear. Having set times for meals, bedtime, and activities provides a sense of security, making it easier for the child to cope with transitions and new experiences. When changes to the routine are inevitable, such as going on a family trip or starting a new school, preparing the child in advance and talking through what to expect can help alleviate anxiety.

Social support is another critical factor in managing anxiety. Children who feel isolated or disconnected from their peers may be more prone to anxiety, especially in social situations. Encouraging the child to engage in activities that promote social interaction, such as joining a club or participating in group sports, can help them build friendships and develop a sense of belonging. It's also important for caregivers to model healthy social behaviors, showing the child how to navigate social interactions with confidence and kindness.

For children who experience anxiety related to academic performance, it can be helpful to work with teachers to create a supportive school environment. This might involve providing accommodations such as extended time on tests, breaks during the school day, or access to a quiet space where the child can go if they feel overwhelmed. Teachers can also play a key role in reinforcing the coping strategies the child is learning at home or in therapy, helping them apply these skills in the classroom.

In some cases, anxiety may be linked to a specific traumatic event, such as a car accident, the death of a loved one, or a natural disaster. For children who have experienced trauma, it's important to provide a safe space where they can process their emotions and fears. Trauma-focused therapy, such as trauma-focused cognitive-behavioral therapy (TF-CBT), can help children work through their trauma in a way that feels manageable and healing.

Children with anxiety often benefit from having a "toolbox" of coping strategies that they can draw from in different situations. This toolbox might include relaxation techniques like deep breathing, a list of positive affirmations, a favorite stuffed animal or comfort object, or a written list of steps they can take when they feel anxious. Having these tools at their disposal helps children feel more in control of their anxiety and better equipped to manage their emotions.

Lastly, it's important for caregivers to take care of their own mental health when supporting a child with anxiety. Parenting an anxious child can be emotionally draining, and caregivers may experience feelings of frustration, helplessness, or guilt. Seeking support from friends, family, or a therapist can provide caregivers with the emotional resources they need to stay calm, patient, and compassionate as they help their child navigate the challenges of anxiety.

The Intersection of Aggression and Anxiety

While aggression and anxiety may seem like opposite behaviors, they are often interconnected. Children who struggle with anxiety may experience heightened levels of frustration, fear, and vulnerability, which can sometimes lead to aggressive outbursts. For example, a child who is anxious about starting a new school may lash out at their peers or siblings as a way of coping with their fear. Similarly, children who are frustrated by their inability to control or understand their anxiety may become aggressive in response to their feelings of helplessness.

Understanding the link between aggression and anxiety can help caregivers address both behaviors in a holistic way. By teaching children emotional regulation skills and providing a safe, supportive environment, caregivers can help reduce both anxiety and aggression, allowing the child to develop healthier ways of expressing their emotions.

For children who experience both aggression and anxiety, it may be helpful to work with a therapist or counselor to develop a comprehensive behavior plan that addresses both issues. This plan might include relaxation techniques to reduce anxiety, cognitive-behavioral strategies to challenge negative thoughts, and social skills training to help the child navigate conflict and frustration without resorting to aggression.

In summary, aggression and anxiety in children are complex but manageable behavioral challenges. Through a combination of emotional regulation techniques, positive reinforcement, professional support, and a nurturing environment, caregivers can help children develop the tools they need to navigate their emotions and build a foundation for long-term emotional health.

Attention-Seeking and Social Challenges

Attention-seeking behavior and social challenges are common issues that many children experience during various stages of development. These behaviors can manifest in different forms and intensities, depending on the child's age, temperament, and environment. Understanding why children engage in attention-seeking behavior and struggle with social challenges is essential for caregivers and educators to help them navigate these difficulties and foster healthy social interactions. In this discussion, we will explore the causes and signs of attention-seeking behavior, the types of social challenges children may encounter, and strategies for addressing these issues effectively.

Attention-seeking behavior is any action a child engages in with the primary goal of gaining attention from adults or peers. This behavior can range from relatively harmless activities, such as interrupting conversations or showing off, to more disruptive actions like tantrums, defiance, or aggression. While it's normal for children to seek attention, especially from parents or caregivers, excessive or problematic attention-seeking behavior often indicates that the child is struggling with unmet emotional or social needs.

Children who engage in attention-seeking behavior may feel neglected, insecure, or anxious, and they use these behaviors as a way to gain validation, reassurance, or control over their environment. It's important to recognize that attention-seeking is not inherently negative; in fact, it's a natural part of human development, as children rely on adult attention for survival, emotional support, and learning. However, when attention-seeking becomes excessive or disruptive, it can interfere with the child's social development and relationships with others.

One of the main causes of attention-seeking behavior is a lack of consistent, positive attention from caregivers. Children who feel ignored or undervalued may resort to attention-seeking as a way to ensure that they are noticed, even if the attention they receive is negative. For example, a child who feels neglected at home may act out in school by interrupting the teacher or disrupting the class in order to receive attention, even if it results in punishment. In this case, the child may view negative attention as preferable to no attention at all.

Another cause of attention-seeking behavior is insecurity or low self-esteem. Children who feel unsure of their abilities or uncertain about their relationships with others may seek attention as a way to gain reassurance or validation. For instance, a child who feels anxious about their social standing may try to impress their peers by showing off or engaging in attention-grabbing behaviors, such as being the class clown or dominating conversations. While these behaviors may temporarily boost the child's confidence, they can ultimately lead to social rejection or conflict with peers.

Attention-seeking behavior can also be a way for children to exert control over their environment. Children who feel powerless or overwhelmed by their circumstances may use attention-seeking as a way to assert themselves and gain a sense of agency. For example, a child who is dealing with stress at home, such as a parental divorce or a new sibling, may act out in order to regain a sense of control and make their needs known. In these cases, the child's behavior is often a reflection of underlying emotional distress that they are unable to articulate.

It's important for caregivers to differentiate between attention-seeking behavior that is developmentally appropriate and behavior that indicates deeper emotional or social challenges. Young children, especially toddlers and preschoolers, naturally seek attention as they learn to navigate their environment and build relationships with adults. This type of attention-seeking is a normal part of development and often diminishes as the child matures and gains more independence. However, if attention-seeking behavior persists into later childhood or becomes disruptive, it may be a sign that the child is struggling with emotional or social difficulties that require intervention.

To address attention-seeking behavior effectively, caregivers should focus on providing consistent, positive attention in a way that meets the child's emotional needs without reinforcing disruptive behavior. One key strategy is to "catch the child being good," meaning that caregivers should actively look for and reinforce positive behaviors, rather than only giving attention when the child is acting out. For example, if a child is playing quietly or following directions, caregivers should acknowledge and praise these behaviors to show the child that they can receive attention for positive actions, not just negative ones.

Another important approach is to set clear expectations and boundaries for behavior. Children who engage in attention-seeking behavior often do so because they are unsure of what is expected of them or because they feel a lack of structure in their environment. By establishing consistent rules and routines, caregivers can provide the child with a sense of security and predictability, reducing the need for attention-seeking behavior. It's also important to follow through with consequences when the child engages in disruptive behaviors, but these consequences should be delivered calmly and without excessive attention to the behavior itself.

Caregivers should also make an effort to provide the child with regular, focused attention in positive ways. This can be as simple as spending a few minutes each day engaging in a shared activity, such as reading a book, playing a game, or having a conversation. By offering the child regular opportunities for connection, caregivers can help reduce the child's need to seek attention through negative behaviors. It's important for caregivers to be fully present during these moments, giving the child their undivided attention and showing interest in their thoughts and feelings.

In addition to addressing attention-seeking behavior, many children also face social challenges that can impact their ability to form healthy relationships with peers. These challenges may include difficulty making friends, social anxiety, conflict resolution issues, or trouble understanding social cues. Social challenges can be particularly difficult for children, as peer relationships are a crucial part of their development and self-identity. Children who struggle socially may feel isolated, rejected, or misunderstood, leading to emotional distress and behavioral problems.

One of the most common social challenges children face is difficulty making and maintaining friendships. Some children may struggle to initiate social interactions, while others may have trouble understanding the give-and-take of friendships, such as sharing, taking turns, or showing empathy. Children who are socially withdrawn or shy may have trouble approaching peers or joining group activities, leading to feelings of loneliness and exclusion. On the other hand, children who are overly assertive or controlling may push their peers away by dominating conversations or insisting on getting their way.

Social anxiety is another common issue that can make it difficult for children to navigate social situations. Children with social anxiety may experience intense fear or discomfort in situations where they are expected to interact with others, such as at school, in group activities, or during playdates. This anxiety can lead to avoidance behaviors, such as refusing to attend social events or staying on the sidelines during group play. Over time, social anxiety can interfere with the child's ability to form meaningful relationships and develop important social skills.

Children who struggle with conflict resolution may also face social challenges, as they may have difficulty managing disagreements or navigating the complexities of peer relationships. These children may react to conflict with aggression, withdrawal, or defiance, rather than using healthy communication strategies to resolve the issue. For example, a child who feels upset because a friend took their toy may respond by hitting or yelling, rather than using words to express their feelings. This can lead to strained relationships and further social difficulties.

Children with developmental or neurological differences, such as autism spectrum disorder (ASD), ADHD, or learning disabilities, may also face unique social challenges. These children may have difficulty reading social cues, understanding nonverbal communication, or recognizing the emotions of others. As a result, they may struggle to form connections with peers or may be perceived as "different" by others, leading to social isolation or bullying. In these cases, targeted social skills training and support from caregivers and educators can be particularly beneficial in helping the child navigate social interactions.

To address social challenges, caregivers and educators can provide children with opportunities to practice and develop social skills in a supportive environment. Role-playing, social stories, and guided play can be effective tools for teaching children how to initiate conversations, take turns, share, and resolve conflicts. For example, caregivers might role-play a scenario where two children want to play with the same toy, helping the child practice using words to negotiate and come up with a solution. Over time, these practice opportunities can help the child build confidence in their social abilities and develop stronger relationships with their peers.

Caregivers should also encourage children to participate in group activities that promote social interaction, such as team sports, clubs, or group games. These activities provide children with structured opportunities to interact with others and practice social skills in a fun and engaging way. For children who are socially anxious or shy, starting with smaller groups or one-on-one interactions may help them feel more comfortable and gradually build their confidence in larger social settings.

It's important for caregivers to model healthy social behaviors in their own interactions. Children learn a great deal about social interactions by observing the adults around them, so caregivers should strive to demonstrate positive communication, empathy, and conflict resolution in their daily lives. For example, if a caregiver is having a disagreement with another adult, they might model active listening, respectful dialogue, and finding a compromise, showing the child how to navigate conflict in a constructive way.

In addition to modeling social behaviors, caregivers can help children develop empathy and emotional awareness by discussing emotions and encouraging perspective-taking. For example, when reading a story or watching a movie, caregivers might ask the child how they think the characters are feeling and why. This helps the child practice recognizing emotions in others and thinking about how their actions affect those around them. Developing empathy is a key component of building positive relationships, as it allows children to understand and respond to the needs and feelings of their peers.

For children with more significant social challenges, such as those with developmental or neurological differences, individualized support from a therapist or social skills group may be necessary. Social skills training can help these children develop the tools they need to navigate social interactions, understand social cues, and build friendships. Therapists may use techniques such as video modeling, social stories, or peer mentoring to teach specific social skills in a way that is tailored to the child's needs.

Caregivers and educators should also be mindful of the potential for bullying or social exclusion, especially for children who struggle with social challenges. Kids who have difficulty fitting in or understanding social norms may become targets for bullying or exclusion, which can further exacerbate their feelings of isolation and anxiety. Caregivers and educators must be vigilant in identifying signs of bullying, such as changes in mood, reluctance to attend school, or withdrawal from social activities, and take immediate action to address the issue.

Preventing bullying starts with creating an inclusive and supportive environment where all children feel valued and accepted. Teachers and caregivers should actively promote kindness, respect, and empathy among all children, encouraging positive interactions and discouraging behaviors that isolate or belittle others. Anti-bullying programs, classroom discussions about inclusion, and peer mentoring can all help foster a culture of acceptance and reduce the likelihood of social exclusion.

For children who have been the victims of bullying or social rejection, it is crucial to provide emotional support and help them rebuild their confidence. Caregivers can help by validating the child's feelings and reassuring them that the bullying is not their fault. At the same time, it's important to teach the child strategies for standing up to bullying, such as seeking help from an adult or using assertive but non-aggressive communication to address the situation.

If a child continues to experience social difficulties or if their social challenges are impacting their emotional well-being, caregivers may want to seek the help of a counselor or therapist. Cognitive-behavioral therapy (CBT), social skills training, and group therapy are all effective interventions for children struggling with social challenges. These therapies provide children with the opportunity to practice social interactions in a structured and supportive setting while developing the emotional resilience needed to handle rejection, conflict, or social anxiety.

Addressing attention-seeking behavior and social challenges requires a multifaceted approach that focuses on building the child's emotional and social skills while providing a safe, supportive environment. It is important to recognize that these behaviors are often driven by underlying emotional needs, such as a desire for connection, a lack of confidence, or difficulty navigating social norms. By addressing these root causes and teaching children healthier ways to seek attention and interact with their peers, caregivers can help them develop the social skills they need to form positive relationships and succeed in social settings.

Another key aspect of helping children overcome attention-seeking behavior and social challenges is teaching them problem-solving and conflict-resolution skills. Children who struggle with social interactions often have difficulty resolving conflicts with peers or navigating complex social dynamics. By teaching children how to communicate effectively, negotiate, and resolve disagreements, caregivers can help them build the tools they need to manage social conflicts without resorting to attention-seeking or disruptive behaviors.

Role-playing is an effective way to teach these skills. Caregivers can set up scenarios where the child practices resolving conflicts in a controlled setting, such as negotiating over a toy or working through a disagreement with a friend. These practice sessions help the child develop confidence in their ability to handle conflicts and can be applied to real-life situations as they arise.

In addition to problem-solving skills, children benefit from learning how to manage their emotions in social situations. Emotional regulation is key to forming and maintaining healthy relationships, as it allows children to navigate social interactions without becoming overwhelmed by frustration, anger, or anxiety. Techniques such as deep breathing, mindfulness, or taking a break when emotions run high can help children stay calm and focused during social interactions, reducing the likelihood of attention-seeking or disruptive behavior.

For children with developmental or neurological differences, social challenges may require additional support from professionals. Social skills groups, often run by therapists or counselors, provide a structured environment where children can practice interacting with peers in a supportive setting. These groups often focus on teaching specific social skills, such as initiating conversations, reading nonverbal cues, or understanding the perspectives of others. By providing children with targeted support in these areas, social skills groups can help them build confidence and improve their social competence over time.

Caregivers should also be mindful of their own role in shaping the child's social development. Children learn a great deal about social interactions by observing the adults around them, so caregivers should model positive social behaviors in their daily interactions. This includes showing kindness, empathy, and respect toward others, as well as demonstrating how to handle conflicts calmly and constructively. When children see these behaviors modeled consistently, they are more likely to adopt them in their own social interactions.

It is also important for caregivers to foster a positive, growth-oriented mindset in children when it comes to social challenges. Rather than focusing on social failures or difficulties, caregivers can encourage children to view challenges as opportunities for growth and learning. For example, if a child struggles to make friends, caregivers can help them reflect on what went well in their social interactions and what they could try differently next time. This approach not only builds resilience but also helps children develop a sense of agency and self-efficacy in social situations.

Encouraging children to participate in extracurricular activities or group settings that align with their interests can also help them build social skills in a less pressured environment. Activities such as sports teams, art classes, or clubs provide children with opportunities to interact with peers who share similar interests, making it easier for them to form connections. These settings often provide a structured environment where social interactions are guided by the activity itself, reducing the social pressure children may feel in unstructured situations.

Finally, caregivers should remember that addressing attention-seeking behavior and social challenges is a gradual process. Children develop at their own pace, and some may take longer than others to build the social skills they need to succeed in peer interactions. It's important to be patient, supportive, and consistent in providing guidance while also celebrating small successes along the way. By creating a nurturing and supportive environment where children feel safe to explore and develop their social skills, caregivers can help them overcome attention-seeking behaviors and social challenges, ultimately leading to healthier relationships and greater emotional well-being.

In conclusion, attention-seeking behavior and social challenges are common but manageable aspects of childhood development. By providing children with the tools they need to express their emotions appropriately, navigate social interactions, and resolve conflicts, caregivers can support their social and emotional growth. With patience, consistency, and a focus on building positive relationships, children can overcome these challenges and develop the confidence and social competence they need to thrive in their relationships with others.

Positive Reinforcement Techniques

Positive reinforcement is one of the most effective and widely used techniques for encouraging desired behavior in children. At its core, positive reinforcement involves providing a reward or some form of acknowledgment immediately after a desired behavior occurs, which increases the likelihood that the behavior will be repeated in the future. This technique, grounded in behavioral psychology, works on the principle that behaviors followed by positive consequences are more likely to be repeated, as the child associates the behavior with a positive outcome. The key to successful positive reinforcement is consistency, timing, and the appropriateness of the reward or praise in relation to the behavior.

Positive reinforcement can be a powerful tool for shaping behavior when applied correctly, but it is important to understand the different types of reinforcement, how to implement them effectively, and the potential pitfalls that can arise when they are used improperly. This chapter will explore the theory behind positive reinforcement, provide practical strategies for using it in various contexts, and discuss how to avoid common mistakes that can undermine its effectiveness.

Positive reinforcement can take many forms, including verbal praise, tangible rewards, extra privileges, or social recognition. The most effective reinforcement depends on the child and the specific situation, as different children respond to different types of rewards. For example, while one child may be motivated by verbal praise, another might prefer earning extra screen time or receiving a small toy. The flexibility of positive reinforcement allows caregivers and educators to tailor their approach to suit the individual needs and preferences of the child, ensuring that the reinforcement is meaningful and motivating.

The principle of positive reinforcement is based on the concept of operant conditioning, a form of learning first described by psychologist B.F. Skinner. In operant conditioning, behaviors are influenced by the consequences that follow them. Positive reinforcement occurs when a behavior is followed by a pleasant or rewarding consequence, which strengthens the behavior and increases the likelihood that it will be repeated. This is in contrast to negative reinforcement, where a behavior is strengthened by the removal of an unpleasant stimulus, and punishment, which is intended to reduce the occurrence of a behavior by introducing an unpleasant consequence.

The use of positive reinforcement in parenting and education has been widely supported by research, as it has been shown to be more effective than punishment in promoting lasting behavioral change. While punishment may stop undesirable behaviors in the short term, it often does not teach the child what to do instead, and it can lead to negative side effects such as fear, resentment, or increased aggression. Positive reinforcement, on the other hand, focuses on encouraging good behavior by teaching children what is expected of them and rewarding them when they meet those expectations. This approach not only fosters better behavior but also helps to build a positive relationship between the child and the caregiver or teacher.

To use positive reinforcement effectively, it is essential to identify the behaviors you want to encourage and to reinforce those behaviors consistently. Children are more likely to repeat behaviors when they receive immediate, positive feedback. For example, if a child is struggling to complete their homework, providing positive reinforcement in the form of praise, a sticker, or extra playtime immediately after they finish their work can motivate them to continue completing their homework in the future. The immediacy of the reinforcement is crucial because it helps the child make a clear connection between the behavior and the reward.

One of the most common forms of positive reinforcement is verbal praise. This can be as simple as saying "Good job!" or "I'm proud of you for sharing." However, for praise to be effective, it must be specific and sincere. Generic praise, such as "Good job," is less effective than specific praise that highlights the behavior you want to reinforce. For example, saying "I really liked the way you helped your brother with his homework" is more impact because it clearly identifies the behavior that is being praised. This helps the child understand exactly what they did well and encourages them to repeat that behavior in the future.

In addition to verbal praise, tangible rewards can also be effective, especially for younger children who may need more concrete reinforcement to understand the connection between their behavior and the reward. Tangible rewards can include stickers, small toys, extra screen time, or special treats. These rewards should be used sparingly and in conjunction with other forms of positive reinforcement, such as praise or privileges, to avoid creating a situation where the child only behaves well in order to receive material rewards. When tangible rewards are used, it's important to ensure that they are appropriate for the behavior being reinforced. For example, a small reward might be appropriate for completing a routine task, such as cleaning up toys, while a larger reward might be reserved for significant achievements, such as mastering a new skill or completing a challenging project.

Another form of positive reinforcement is the use of privileges, such as allowing the child extra playtime, giving them control over a family decision (like choosing what's for dinner), or allowing them to stay up a little later on weekends. Privileges can be especially effective for older children, as they often appreciate the increased autonomy and responsibility that comes with these rewards. Like other forms of reinforcement, privileges should be used in a way that is consistent and tied to specific behaviors, so that the child understands what they are earning and why.

It's important to remember that positive reinforcement doesn't always have to come from adults; peer recognition can also be a powerful motivator, particularly for older children and adolescents. Social recognition, such as being praised by classmates for good behavior or being chosen as a team leader, can boost a child's self-esteem and encourage them to continue exhibiting positive behaviors. Group-based reinforcement systems, such as classroom reward charts or team-based incentives, can also be effective in promoting positive behavior in a social context.

While positive reinforcement is highly effective, there are potential pitfalls that caregivers and educators should be aware of to avoid diminishing its impact. One common mistake is over-reliance on material rewards, which can lead to a situation where the child expects to be rewarded for every small behavior. This can undermine the intrinsic motivation to behave well and create a dependency on external rewards. To avoid this, caregivers should use material rewards sparingly and focus on using verbal praise, privileges, and social recognition as primary forms of reinforcement.

Another potential pitfall is inconsistency in the application of reinforcement. Positive reinforcement is most effective when it is applied consistently, meaning that desired behaviors are always followed by a positive consequence. If reinforcement is only given sporadically or if different caregivers apply different rules, the child may become confused about what behaviors are expected of them and may not consistently exhibit the desired behavior. Consistency across all caregivers, whether parents, teachers, or other adults, is key to ensuring that the child receives clear and predictable feedback about their behavior.

It's also important to avoid reinforcing undesired behaviors inadvertently. For example, if a child throws a tantrum in a store and is given a treat to calm them down, the child may learn that tantrums are an effective way to get what they want. This is an example of negative reinforcement, where the removal of an unpleasant stimulus (the tantrum) reinforces the child's behavior. To avoid this, caregivers should be mindful of how they respond to undesired behaviors and ensure that they are not unintentionally rewarding them.

One of the challenges of using positive reinforcement is finding the right balance between reinforcing desired behaviors and not over-rewarding behaviors that should be expected as part of daily routines. For example, while it's appropriate to reward a child for going above and beyond, such as helping a sibling without being asked, it's also important to teach children that some behaviors, like brushing their teeth or cleaning up after themselves, are simply expected parts of being responsible and don't always require a reward. Over time, as children internalize these behaviors, the frequency of reinforcement can be reduced, helping them transition from extrinsic motivation (being motivated by rewards) to intrinsic motivation (being motivated by personal satisfaction or a sense of accomplishment).

Positive reinforcement is also an excellent tool for addressing specific behavioral challenges or encouraging the development of new skills. For children who struggle with specific issues, such as completing homework, following directions, or managing emotions, caregivers can use targeted reinforcement strategies to help them improve in these areas. For example, a child who struggles with homework might be given a sticker for every 15 minutes of focused work, with a larger reward earned after a week of consistent effort. Over time, the reinforcement can be gradually phased out as the child becomes more confident and capable of completing the task independently.

For children with developmental or behavioral challenges, such as ADHD or autism spectrum disorder, positive reinforcement can be particularly effective when used as part of a structured behavior plan. In these cases, caregivers and educators may work with behavioral therapists to develop individualized reinforcement strategies that are tailored to the child's specific needs. For example, a child with ADHD who has difficulty sitting still during class might receive a token for every 10 minutes of focused behavior, with the tokens being exchanged for a reward at the end of the day. These structured reinforcement systems help children build the skills they need to succeed while providing clear and consistent feedback about their progress.

It's also important to remember that positive reinforcement is not just about modifying behavior; it's about building relationships and creating a positive, supportive environment where children feel valued and understood. When children receive positive reinforcement, they not only learn what behaviors are expected of them, but they also develop a sense of competence and self-worth. This, in turn, helps to build a strong foundation for future learning and development.

In conclusion, positive reinforcement is a powerful and versatile tool for encouraging desired behaviors and promoting positive development in children. By providing consistent, timely, and meaningful reinforcement, caregivers and educators can help children internalize good behaviors, develop new skills, and build a strong sense of self-efficacy. Whether through verbal praise, tangible rewards, privileges, or social recognition, positive reinforcement provides children with the motivation and encouragement they need to thrive both at home and in the classroom.

Time-Outs and Emotional Regulation

Time-outs and emotional regulation are two intertwined strategies used by caregivers and educators to help children manage their behavior and emotions effectively. Time-outs are a behavioral management technique that, when implemented correctly, can help children calm down, reflect on their actions, and regain control of their emotions. Emotional regulation, on the other hand, is the broader skill of managing and responding to emotions in a healthy and appropriate manner. Both techniques work together to promote self-discipline and emotional intelligence in children, fostering their ability to handle frustration, anger, and other intense emotions in constructive ways.

Time-outs are often misunderstood and misused. When people hear the term "time-out," they may envision it as a punishment in which a child is isolated from others, perhaps sent to a corner or a quiet room to sit alone. However, time-outs should not be seen purely as punitive measures. Rather, when used correctly, they are a tool for giving the child a break from a challenging situation, allowing them the space to calm down and regain their composure. The goal of a time-out is not to punish the child but to help them disengage from a problematic behavior and create an opportunity to reflect on what has happened.

The effectiveness of time-outs relies heavily on how and when they are implemented. The primary purpose of a time-out is to help the child regulate their emotions and behaviors, so it's crucial that caregivers approach time-outs with patience and consistency. Time-outs should be seen as part of a broader strategy for teaching emotional regulation and problem-solving skills, rather than as an isolated form of discipline. For this reason, time-outs should always be paired with follow-up discussions or teaching moments where the child can process their feelings and understand how to better handle similar situations in the future.

One of the most important aspects of using time-outs effectively is ensuring that the child understands why they are being given a time-out. Children need to know what behavior led to the time-out, so it is essential for caregivers to explain this clearly and calmly. For instance, if a child is acting aggressively towards a sibling, the caregiver might say, "You're hitting your brother, so I'm giving you a time-out to calm down." This provides the child with immediate feedback about their behavior and the reason for the time-out. It's also important for the caregiver to explain that the time-out is an opportunity to calm down, not a punishment in the traditional sense.

Timing is another critical factor when using time-outs. The length of the time-out should be appropriate to the child's age and attention span. A common guideline is to give one minute of time-out per year of age, so a five-year-old might have a five-minute time-out, while a seven-year-old might have a seven-minute time-out. However, this is not a strict rule, and caregivers should be flexible depending on the situation and the child's individual needs. The goal is to give the child enough time to calm down without feeling isolated or punished for an excessive amount of time. If the child is still upset after the time-out has ended, the caregiver may need to extend the time-out or provide additional support to help the child regain emotional control.

The environment in which the time-out takes place is also important. Ideally, the time-out should occur in a quiet, neutral space that is free from distractions. This space should not be punitive in nature; for example, sending a child to their room full of toys might not be effective, as the child could become distracted and fail to reflect on their behavior. On the other hand, sending a child to a dark, isolated space could foster feelings of fear or resentment, which undermines the purpose of the time-out. The goal is to create a space where the child can sit calmly and reflect on their actions without feeling punished or overwhelmed.

After the time-out has ended, it's important to follow up with a discussion to help the child process what happened and learn from the experience. This discussion should be calm and supportive, focusing on the child's emotions and how they can handle similar situations in the future. For example, a caregiver might say, "I know you were feeling really angry when you hit your brother. Can we talk about what made you so upset?" This allows the child to express their feelings and helps them understand that it's okay to feel angry, but it's not okay to act aggressively. The caregiver can then offer suggestions for alternative behaviors, such as using words to express frustration or taking deep breaths to calm down.

The process of teaching emotional regulation goes hand in hand with using time-outs. Emotional regulation is the ability to recognize, understand, and manage one's emotions in a healthy way. Children are not born with fully developed emotional regulation skills; they must be taught how to manage their feelings, especially when they are upset, frustrated, or overwhelmed. Time-outs can serve as a tool for helping children practice emotional regulation, as they provide a structured opportunity for the child to step away from a situation, calm down, and reflect on their emotions.

One of the key components of emotional regulation is teaching children to identify their emotions. Young children may not always have the vocabulary to describe how they are feeling, which can lead to frustration and acting out. Caregivers can help by labeling emotions for the child and modeling how to express feelings appropriately. For example, if a child is upset because they didn't get their way, the caregiver might say, "It seems like you're feeling disappointed because you wanted that toy. It's okay to feel disappointed, but it's not okay to scream." This helps the child put words to their emotions and understand that it's normal to feel upset, but they need to express their feelings in a way that doesn't hurt others or disrupt the environment.

Another important aspect of emotional regulation is teaching children coping strategies for managing strong emotions. Time-outs can be an opportunity for children to practice these strategies. For instance, a caregiver might encourage a child to take deep breaths, count to ten, or practice mindfulness techniques during a time-out. These strategies help the child calm down in the moment and can be used outside of time-outs to prevent emotional outbursts in the future. Over time, children learn to use these techniques on their own, which fosters greater independence in managing their emotions.

Consistency is crucial when teaching emotional regulation. Children need to know that there are clear expectations for their behavior and that caregivers will respond in a consistent manner when those expectations are not met. If time-outs are used sporadically or inconsistently, children may become confused about what is expected of them and how they are supposed to manage their emotions. It's important for all caregivers—whether parents, teachers, or other adults—to be on the same page when it comes to using time-outs and teaching emotional regulation. This consistency helps children internalize the rules and expectations, making it easier for them to regulate their emotions and behaviors over time.

While time-outs and emotional regulation strategies are effective for many children, it's important to recognize that they may not work for every child in every situation. Some children, particularly those with developmental or neurological differences such as autism spectrum disorder (ASD) or ADHD, may struggle with emotional regulation in ways that require additional support. For these children, time-outs may need to be adapted to meet their individual needs. For example, a child with ADHD might benefit from a shorter time-out with a clear, structured activity to help them refocus their attention, while a child with ASD might need a sensory-friendly space for time-outs to prevent sensory overload.

In some cases, children may exhibit extreme emotional reactions that go beyond the scope of typical time-out strategies. For children who frequently struggle with emotional dysregulation or who have difficulty calming down even after time-outs, it may be necessary to seek additional support from a therapist or counselor. Cognitive-behavioral therapy (CBT), for example, can be highly effective in helping children develop emotional regulation skills. A therapist can work with the child to identify triggers for emotional outbursts, develop coping strategies, and practice using these skills in a supportive environment.

It's also important for caregivers to model emotional regulation in their own behavior. Children learn a great deal from observing the adults around them, and caregivers who demonstrate calm, controlled responses to stress and frustration can serve as powerful role models for children. For example, if a caregiver is feeling frustrated by a child's behavior, they might say, "I'm feeling really frustrated right now, so I'm going to take a few deep breaths to calm down." This shows the child that it's okay to feel strong emotions, but there are healthy ways to manage those feelings without acting out.

In addition to modeling emotional regulation, caregivers can create a supportive environment where children feel safe to express their emotions. It's important for children to know that all emotions—whether positive or negative—are valid and that they won't be judged or punished for expressing how they feel. When children feel safe to talk about their emotions, they are more likely to seek help when they're struggling and to develop the emotional intelligence needed to navigate difficult situations.

Building emotional regulation skills is a long-term process, and it requires patience, consistency, and support from caregivers. Time-outs are just one tool in this process, and they should be used as part of a broader approach that includes teaching children how to identify their emotions, providing them with coping strategies, and modeling healthy emotional responses. When used effectively, time-outs can help children develop the self-discipline and emotional intelligence needed to succeed in school, relationships, and other aspects of life.

To support the development of emotional regulation, caregivers can also use positive reinforcement to encourage children when they handle their emotions appropriately. For example, if a child uses deep breathing to calm down instead of throwing a tantrum, the caregiver might praise the child by saying, "I'm really proud of you for taking deep breaths when you were upset." This reinforces the behavior and encourages the child to continue using healthy coping strategies in the future.

In conclusion, time-outs and emotional regulation are essential tools for helping children learn how to manage their emotions and behavior in a healthy and constructive way. By incorporating these techniques into daily routines, caregivers can create a supportive environment where children feel empowered to manage their emotions, make better choices, and develop self-discipline. The combination of time-outs and emotional regulation strategies lays the groundwork for children to handle frustration, anger, and other intense emotions in ways that benefit both themselves and those around them.

In order to make time-outs and emotional regulation strategies even more effective, caregivers can create clear expectations about what will happen during a time-out. For instance, before a time-out is implemented, the caregiver might explain to the child, "During a time-out, you will sit quietly and calm your body and mind. This is a time for you to take a break, not to play or get upset further." Having these expectations in place ensures that the child understands what a time-out entails and helps them use the time productively to self-regulate.

An additional technique that can be used to enhance time-out effectiveness is providing the child with tools or techniques they can use while in time-out to help them calm down. These might include fidget toys, stress balls, or calming visual aids, such as sensory bottles filled with glitter or sand. Giving the child something tangible to focus on during the time-out can help them engage in self-soothing and make the process of calming down more manageable, especially for children who may have difficulty sitting still or who struggle with sensory processing issues.

Moreover, caregivers can establish "calm-down routines" that the child can practice during or after the time-out. This routine might include taking deep breaths, visualizing a peaceful place, counting to ten, or engaging in light physical movement, such as stretching. These activities not only help the child calm down during the time-out, but they also teach them valuable emotional regulation skills that they can use outside of the time-out context. By practicing these routines consistently, the child becomes better equipped to manage their emotions in real-time, without needing to rely solely on external cues from caregivers.

The success of time-outs and emotional regulation techniques depends largely on the relationship between the caregiver and the child. Children are more likely to accept and benefit from time-outs when they feel a strong connection to the caregiver and when the time-out is framed as an opportunity for growth rather than as punishment. For this reason, caregivers should approach time-outs with empathy and understanding, rather than frustration or anger. Instead of viewing the time-out as a punitive measure, it should be seen as a moment for the child to regroup and regain control over their emotions, while also fostering communication and emotional awareness.

It's also important for caregivers to acknowledge the child's emotions after a time-out is over. Children need to know that their feelings are valid, even if their behavior was inappropriate. This validation helps the child understand that it's okay to feel upset, but it's not okay to hurt others or act out destructively. For instance, a caregiver might say, "I understand that you were very frustrated when your sister took your toy, and it's okay to feel angry. But hitting isn't the right way to handle that feeling. Next time, try using your words to tell her how you feel." This type of conversation reinforces emotional awareness while offering alternative ways of responding to challenging situations.

Caregivers should also be open to listening to the child's perspective after a time-out, especially as the child becomes older and more capable of expressing themselves. Giving the child the opportunity to explain their feelings and thoughts about the situation that led to the time-out can promote a sense of agency and help the child feel heard and understood. This can turn the time-out into a learning experience where both the caregiver and the child reflect on what happened and how things can be handled differently in the future. This approach not only strengthens the caregiver-child relationship but also fosters problem-solving skills in the child.

Consistency is a key component of both time-outs and emotional regulation. Children need to know that certain behaviors will consistently lead to time-outs and that they will have opportunities to calm down and reflect after each time-out. Caregivers who apply time-outs inconsistently—sometimes giving a time-out for a behavior and other times not—can confuse the child and make it harder for them to learn from the experience. Likewise, being consistent with emotional regulation strategies, such as reminding the child to use their coping skills or modeling emotional regulation in the caregiver's own behavior, helps the child internalize these skills over time.

As children grow and develop, caregivers should adjust their use of time-outs and emotional regulation strategies to suit the child's evolving needs. For younger children, time-outs may need to be more frequent and closely monitored, while older children may benefit from more independent forms of emotional regulation, such as taking a break on their own or using a self-calming routine without being prompted. Over time, the goal is for the child to develop enough emotional regulation skills that they no longer need to rely on external time-outs as frequently, but can instead regulate their emotions in real-time and respond to challenges with greater self-control.

In addition, caregivers can integrate emotional literacy into everyday life by talking openly about emotions and encouraging the child to express their feelings regularly. This practice helps normalize conversations about emotions, making it easier for the child to recognize and label their emotions in the moment, rather than allowing their feelings to build up and lead to emotional outbursts. The more comfortable a child becomes with talking about their feelings, the easier it will be for them to use emotional regulation techniques to manage those feelings effectively.

Schools and educational environments can also play a crucial role in supporting emotional regulation and the appropriate use of time-outs. Teachers and school staff can collaborate with caregivers to ensure that consistent strategies are used at home and in the classroom. When both caregivers and educators are on the same page, children receive consistent messages about behavior expectations and emotional regulation. In school settings, teachers can create "calm-down corners" or designated spaces where students can go to take a break when they feel overwhelmed. These spaces are not punitive but provide an opportunity for students to self-regulate before re-engaging with the class.

For children with special needs, such as those with autism spectrum disorder (ASD), ADHD, or other behavioral challenges, time-outs and emotional regulation strategies may need to be adapted to meet their specific requirements. These children may require additional support to understand and process their emotions, and they may benefit from visual aids, sensory tools, or more structured routines to help them calm down. Caregivers and educators should work closely with specialists, such as occupational therapists or behavioral therapists, to develop individualized strategies that support emotional regulation in children with special needs.

In some cases, it may be necessary to combine time-outs and emotional regulation strategies with professional interventions, such as therapy or counseling. Children who struggle with severe emotional dysregulation or who frequently experience intense emotional outbursts may benefit from working with a therapist who can help them develop additional coping strategies. Cognitive-behavioral therapy (CBT) is one evidence-based approach that can be highly effective in helping children identify and challenge unhelpful thought patterns that contribute to emotional dysregulation.

Overall, time-outs and emotional regulation are not about punishment but about teaching children how to manage their emotions in a healthy and constructive way. These strategies provide children with the tools they need to navigate challenging emotions, build resilience, and develop self-control. By using time-outs in a calm, consistent manner and supporting children in learning emotional regulation techniques, caregivers can foster emotional intelligence, self-awareness, and long-term behavioral success in children. The combination of these techniques sets the stage for children to grow into emotionally capable individuals who can handle life's challenges with confidence and composure.

Communication and Conflict Resolution

Effective communication and conflict resolution are essential skills for children to develop as they grow and navigate social relationships with family, peers, and authority figures. Teaching these skills at an early age fosters better emotional regulation, problem-solving abilities, and helps children build strong, healthy relationships. Communication and conflict resolution are interconnected; without clear communication, resolving conflicts becomes much more difficult, as misunderstandings, frustration, and unspoken feelings can easily escalate into larger issues.

Children are not born with the innate ability to communicate effectively or to resolve conflicts peacefully. These are learned skills, developed through observation, practice, and guidance from caregivers and educators. The process of learning these skills takes time, patience, and consistent modeling from adults, who play a critical role in helping children understand how to express themselves and how to handle disagreements in a constructive way. By teaching these skills early, caregivers help children avoid common pitfalls like aggression, avoidance, or passive behaviors in conflict situations, setting the foundation for positive social interactions throughout their lives.

At its core, communication involves not only speaking but also listening, understanding nonverbal cues, and empathizing with others. For children, learning to communicate effectively means learning how to express their needs, feelings, and thoughts clearly, while also developing the ability to listen to others with respect and empathy. It requires an understanding of verbal and nonverbal communication, including body language, tone of voice, and facial expressions, all of which convey important information in social interactions.

Conflict resolution is the process by which disagreements or disputes are managed in a way that minimizes negative outcomes and fosters understanding and cooperation. Conflicts arise naturally in any social setting, whether at home, in school, or during play. Teaching children how to resolve conflicts peacefully and constructively helps them navigate the inevitable disagreements that will arise in their relationships, both during childhood and later in life. Conflict resolution skills involve recognizing the problem, communicating clearly and respectfully, identifying possible solutions, and working toward a mutually agreeable outcome.

One of the first steps in teaching children effective communication is helping them develop emotional literacy—the ability to recognize, label, and express their emotions. Young children, especially, may struggle to communicate their feelings because they lack the vocabulary or understanding to do so. As a result, they may act out in frustration or become withdrawn when they don't know how to express their emotions verbally. Caregivers can support the development of emotional literacy by helping children identify and name their feelings, using simple language to explain emotions. For example, a caregiver might say, "I see you're feeling angry because you didn't get a turn with the toy. It's okay to feel angry, but let's talk about it instead of hitting." This approach validates the child's feelings while guiding them toward healthier ways of expressing their emotions.

In addition to teaching children to express their emotions, caregivers must also help children learn to listen actively. Active listening means paying full attention to the speaker, showing empathy, and responding thoughtfully. It involves both verbal and nonverbal cues—nodding, making eye contact, and paraphrasing what the speaker has said to ensure understanding. For children, learning to listen attentively is crucial because it helps them understand the perspectives and needs of others, which is a key component of resolving conflicts. Caregivers can model active listening by giving their full attention to children when they are speaking, asking clarifying questions, and showing empathy. For example, if a child is upset about something that happened at school, the caregiver might say, "It sounds like you were really disappointed when your friend didn't want to play with you. How did that make you feel?"

As children develop their communication skills, it's important to teach them how to express their needs and opinions assertively, rather than passively or aggressively. Assertive communication means speaking up for oneself in a way that is respectful and clear, without being aggressive or disrespectful. It involves using "I" statements, such as "I feel upset when you take my toys without asking," rather than accusatory "you" statements like "You're always taking my stuff!" Assertive communication helps prevent misunderstandings and escalations, as it focuses on the speaker's feelings and needs without blaming or attacking the other person. Caregivers can role-play different scenarios with children to help them practice assertive communication, offering guidance on how to express their feelings calmly and respectfully.

Nonverbal communication is another critical aspect of effective communication, and it's important for children to learn how to read and interpret nonverbal cues. Body language, facial expressions, and tone of voice can convey as much, if not more, than words in social interactions. For example, a child may say they are "fine," but their slumped posture, frowning face, or crossed arms may suggest otherwise. Teaching children to recognize these cues in themselves and others can help them navigate social situations more effectively and avoid misunderstandings. Caregivers can point out nonverbal cues during everyday interactions, asking the child questions like, "How do you think your friend is feeling right now? What can you tell from the way they're standing or the look on their face?"

Along with communication, conflict resolution is a vital skill for children to learn. Conflicts are inevitable in any social setting, whether at home, school, or among friends. Rather than avoiding conflicts or allowing them to escalate into physical or emotional outbursts, children can be taught to approach disagreements with a problem-solving mindset. This involves helping children understand that conflict is a normal part of relationships and that there are ways to resolve disagreements that are fair and respectful to everyone involved.

One of the first steps in conflict resolution is teaching children to recognize when a conflict is happening and to identify the source of the disagreement. This can be challenging for young children, who may not always understand why they are upset or why a conflict has occurred. Caregivers can help by asking guiding questions, such as, "What happened that made you feel upset?" or "Why do you think your friend is upset?" This encourages children to reflect on the situation and identify the underlying issue, rather than focusing solely on their emotional reaction.

Once the source of the conflict has been identified, the next step is teaching children to express their feelings and needs clearly. This ties back to the communication skills discussed earlier—using "I" statements and speaking assertively. For example, if two children are arguing over a toy, one child might say, "I feel frustrated when you take the toy without asking. I would like a turn, too." By encouraging children to express their needs in a calm and clear way, caregivers help prevent the conflict from escalating and create an opportunity for resolution.

After both sides have expressed their feelings and needs, the next step in conflict resolution is brainstorming possible solutions. This involves helping children think creatively about how the conflict can be resolved in a way that is fair to both parties. Caregivers can guide this process by asking open-ended questions like, "What do you think we could do to make sure everyone gets a turn?" or "How can we solve this problem so that everyone feels happy?" By involving children in the problem-solving process, caregivers encourage them to take ownership of the solution and develop critical thinking skills that will serve them well in future conflicts.

It's important to emphasize that conflict resolution is not about winning or losing, but about finding a solution that works for everyone involved. This can be a difficult concept for young children to grasp, especially when they are used to thinking in terms of fairness as "equal shares" or "taking turns." Caregivers can help shift this mindset by focusing on the idea of compromise—finding a solution that meets the needs of both parties, even if it doesn't give everyone exactly what they want. For example, if two children both want to play with the same toy, a compromise might involve taking turns or finding a different game they can play together.

Once a solution has been agreed upon, it's important for caregivers to follow up and ensure that the resolution is being implemented and that both parties feel satisfied with the outcome. This helps reinforce the idea that conflict resolution is an ongoing process and that it's important to check in with others after a disagreement to make sure the problem has been fully resolved. For example, after two children have agreed to take turns with a toy, the caregiver might check in after a few minutes to ask, "How's it going? Are you both getting a chance to play?" This follow-up reinforces the idea that conflict resolution is about cooperation and maintaining positive relationships.

Another key aspect of teaching conflict resolution is helping children develop empathy and perspective-taking skills. In many conflicts, the root cause is a lack of understanding or consideration for the other person's feelings or point of view. By teaching children to think about how others are feeling and to consider the impact of their actions, caregivers can help reduce the likelihood of conflicts arising in the first place. For example, if a child takes a toy from a friend without asking, the caregiver might say, "How do you think your friend feels when you take the toy without asking? What could you do differently next time?" This encourages the child to put themselves in the other person's shoes and think about how their actions affect others.

COMMUNICATION AND CONFLICT RESOLUTION

In addition to teaching empathy, caregivers can also model effective conflict resolution in their own interactions. Children learn a great deal by observing the adults around them, so it's important for caregivers to demonstrate how to handle disagreements calmly and constructively. For example, if two adults have a disagreement in front of a child, they can model respectful communication by listening to each other, expressing their feelings without blaming, and working together to find a solution. By seeing conflict resolution in action, children learn that disagreements don't have to be scary or combative—they can be opportunities for growth and understanding.

It's also important to teach children that conflict resolution doesn't always mean everyone will get exactly what they want. Sometimes, the best solution is one that requires compromise or accepting that the outcome won't be perfect for everyone. Caregivers can help children understand this by framing conflicts as opportunities to practice fairness, cooperation, and problem-solving, rather than as competitions to be won. The goal in conflict resolution should be to foster understanding, empathy, and a shared sense of cooperation, rather than focusing solely on personal victory. For instance, if two children are arguing over a game, caregivers can highlight that even though both might not get their first choice, they can still enjoy playing together by agreeing on a different game. This shift in mindset from "winning" to "working together" helps children develop a more collaborative and less adversarial approach to conflict.

To reinforce these lessons, caregivers can introduce the concept of "win-win" solutions. In a win-win situation, both parties feel that their needs have been acknowledged and respected, even if they don't get exactly what they initially wanted. For example, if two children are fighting over a single toy, a win-win solution might involve agreeing to play a different game together for now and then switching to the toy later, ensuring both children feel their preferences are taken into account. By framing conflict resolution as an opportunity to create win-win outcomes, children learn that conflicts don't have to end with one person being satisfied and the other feeling left out.

When it comes to teaching conflict resolution, role-playing is an especially effective tool. Role-playing allows children to practice managing conflicts in a safe and controlled environment before they encounter real-life disagreements. Caregivers can set up various scenarios that mimic common conflicts children might face, such as disagreements over toys, taking turns, or dealing with teasing from peers. By guiding children through the process of resolving these conflicts, caregivers help them build confidence in their problem-solving abilities and reinforce the communication and empathy skills needed to resolve real-world disputes.

It's also important to celebrate and acknowledge when children successfully navigate a conflict or use effective communication skills. Positive reinforcement, such as praising the child for how they handled a disagreement or pointing out their efforts in listening and compromising, helps solidify these skills. For instance, a caregiver might say, "I'm really proud of how you and your sister worked together to figure out a way to share the toys. You both did a great job listening to each other." This not only reinforces the behavior but also helps the child associate conflict resolution with positive outcomes and a sense of accomplishment.

In addition to helping children manage conflicts with peers, caregivers should also teach children how to handle conflicts with authority figures, such as parents, teachers, or other adults. While it's important for children to learn to respect authority, it's also crucial for them to understand that they have the right to express their feelings and opinions, even in situations where there is a power imbalance. Teaching children to respectfully voice their concerns when they feel unfairly treated, rather than bottling up their feelings or acting out aggressively, is an important part of conflict resolution. For example, if a child feels that a rule is unfair, caregivers can encourage them to express their concerns calmly, using respectful language like, "I don't think it's fair that I'm the only one who has to clean up. Can we talk about it?"

This teaches children that conflicts with authority figures don't have to be confrontational or result in punishment. Instead, these moments can serve as opportunities for open dialogue and mutual understanding. When children feel heard and respected, they are more likely to follow rules and accept guidance, even when they don't fully agree with every decision made by an authority figure.

It's also valuable to acknowledge that sometimes, conflicts don't get fully resolved. Not every disagreement will end with everyone feeling satisfied, and that's okay. Part of conflict resolution is learning how to cope with disappointment and accepting that not all outcomes will be ideal. This is another area where emotional regulation comes into play. Caregivers can help children manage their feelings of disappointment or frustration by teaching them coping strategies, such as taking deep breaths, using positive self-talk, or engaging in a calming activity. For example, if a child is upset because they didn't get their way during a disagreement, the caregiver might say, "I know you're disappointed, and it's okay to feel that way. Let's take a few deep breaths and think about something else we can do together."

Developing these coping mechanisms helps children manage their emotional reactions to conflicts and prevents negative behaviors like sulking, aggression, or withdrawal. It also reinforces the idea that while conflicts are a natural part of life, they don't have to result in ongoing resentment or anger. By teaching children how to manage unresolved conflicts with grace and emotional resilience, caregivers set the stage for healthier, more adaptive social interactions in the future.

Schools play a significant role in supporting children's development of communication and conflict resolution skills. Teachers and school staff can reinforce the skills children learn at home by creating a classroom environment that encourages respectful communication and cooperative problem-solving. Classroom activities, such as group projects or peer mediation programs, provide opportunities for children to practice resolving conflicts in a structured and supportive setting. Peer mediation programs, in particular, are effective in teaching students how to handle conflicts on their own, with the guidance of trained student mediators who facilitate discussions between peers. This not only helps resolve specific conflicts but also fosters a culture of respect and understanding within the school community.

Teachers can also model effective communication and conflict resolution in their interactions with students, showing children how to handle disagreements or challenges with empathy, patience, and fairness. By observing adults using these skills, children learn that even in difficult situations, it's possible to maintain respectful, open communication and work toward positive solutions.

For children with special needs, such as those with autism spectrum disorder (ASD) or ADHD, communication and conflict resolution may require additional support and tailored strategies. These children may struggle with reading social cues, understanding nonverbal communication, or managing their emotions during conflicts. Caregivers and educators should work closely with therapists or specialists to develop individualized approaches that meet the child's specific needs. For example, children with ASD might benefit from visual supports or social stories that help them understand different social situations and how to respond appropriately. In these cases, teaching communication and conflict resolution may require more repetition and structured practice, but with the right support, these children can still develop the skills they need to navigate social interactions successfully.

It's important to note that conflict resolution is a lifelong skill that continues to develop as children grow into adolescents and adults. The foundation laid in early childhood—through the consistent modeling and teaching of communication and conflict resolution skills—prepares children for the more complex conflicts they will face as they mature. Adolescents, in particular, may encounter new types of conflicts related to peer pressure, identity, or more significant interpersonal disputes. The skills they learned in childhood provide a crucial framework for handling these challenges in a constructive and emotionally healthy way.

For older children and teenagers, it's important to continue encouraging open communication and reinforcing conflict resolution strategies, while also respecting their growing independence. Adolescents may need more autonomy in resolving their conflicts, but caregivers should remain available to provide guidance and support when needed. This balance between independence and support helps teenagers feel confident in their ability to manage conflicts while knowing they have a trusted adult to turn to if they need help.

In summary, teaching communication and conflict resolution skills to children is an ongoing process that requires patience, modeling, and consistent practice. These skills not only help children navigate the social challenges of childhood but also lay the foundation for healthy, respectful relationships throughout their lives. By focusing on clear communication, empathy, and cooperative problem-solving, caregivers and educators can help children develop the tools they need to resolve conflicts peacefully and build strong, positivrather than as competitions to be won. The goal in conflict resolution should be to foster understanding, empathy, and a shared sense of cooperation, rather than focusing solely on personal victory. For instance, if two children are arguing over a game, caregivers can highlight that even though both might not get their first choice, they can still enjoy playing together by agreeing on a different game. This shift in mindset from "winning" to "working together" helps children develop a more collaborative and less adversarial approach to conflict.

To reinforce these lessons, caregivers can introduce the concept of "win-win" solutions. In a win-win situation, both parties feel that their needs have been acknowledged and respected, even if they don't get exactly what they initially wanted. For example, if two children are fighting over a single toy, a win-win solution might involve agreeing to play a different game together for now and then switching to the toy later, ensuring both children feel their preferences are taken into account. By framing conflict resolution as an opportunity to create win-win outcomes, children learn that conflicts don't have to end with one person being satisfied and the other feeling left out.

When it comes to teaching conflict resolution, role-playing is an especially effective tool. Role-playing allows children to practice managing conflicts in a safe and controlled environment before they encounter real-life disagreements. Caregivers can set up various scenarios that mimic common conflicts children might face, such as disagreements over toys, taking turns, or dealing with teasing from peers. By guiding children through the process of resolving these conflicts, caregivers help them build confidence in their problem-solving abilities and reinforce the communication and empathy skills needed to resolve real-world disputes.

It's also important to celebrate and acknowledge when children successfully navigate a conflict or use effective communication skills. Positive reinforcement, such as praising the child for how they handled a disagreement or pointing out their efforts in listening and compromising, helps solidify these skills. For instance, a caregiver might say, "I'm really proud of how you and your sister worked together to figure out a way to share the toys. You both did a great job listening to each other." This not only reinforces the behavior but also helps the child associate conflict resolution with positive outcomes and a sense of accomplishment.

In addition to helping children manage conflicts with peers, caregivers should also teach children how to handle conflicts with authority figures, such as parents, teachers, or other adults. While it's important for children to learn to respect authority, it's also crucial for them to understand that they have the right to express their feelings and opinions, even in situations where there is a power imbalance. Teaching children to respectfully voice their concerns when they feel unfairly treated, rather than bottling up their feelings or acting out aggressively, is an important part of conflict resolution. For example, if a child feels that a rule is unfair, caregivers can encourage them to express their concerns calmly, using respectful language like, "I don't think it's fair that I'm the only one who has to clean up. Can we talk about it?"

This teaches children that conflicts with authority figures don't have to be confrontational or result in punishment. Instead, these moments can serve as opportunities for open dialogue and mutual understanding. When children feel heard and respected, they are more likely to follow rules and accept guidance, even when they don't fully agree with every decision made by an authority figure.

It's also valuable to acknowledge that sometimes, conflicts don't get fully resolved. Not every disagreement will end with everyone feeling satisfied, and that's okay. Part of conflict resolution is learning how to cope with disappointment and accepting that not all outcomes will be ideal. This is another area where emotional regulation comes into play. Caregivers can help children manage their feelings of disappointment or frustration by teaching them coping strategies, such as taking deep breaths, using positive self-talk, or engaging in a calming activity. For example, if a child is upset because they didn't get their way during a disagreement, the caregiver might say, "I know you're disappointed, and it's okay to feel that way. Let's take a few deep breaths and think about something else we can do together."

Developing these coping mechanisms helps children manage their emotional reactions to conflicts and prevents negative behaviors like sulking, aggression, or withdrawal. It also reinforces the idea that while conflicts are a natural part of life, they don't have to result in ongoing resentment or anger. By teaching children how to manage unresolved conflicts with grace and emotional resilience, caregivers set the stage for healthier, more adaptive social interactions in the future.

Schools play a significant role in supporting children's development of communication and conflict resolution skills. Teachers and school staff can reinforce the skills children learn at home by creating a classroom environment that encourages respectful communication and cooperative problem-solving. Classroom activities, such as group projects or peer mediation programs, provide opportunities for children to practice resolving conflicts in a structured and supportive setting. Peer mediation programs, in particular, are effective in teaching students how to handle conflicts on their own, with the guidance of trained student mediators who facilitate discussions between peers. This not only helps resolve specific conflicts but also fosters a culture of respect and understanding within the school community.

Teachers can also model effective communication and conflict resolution in their interactions with students, showing children how to handle disagreements or challenges with empathy, patience, and fairness. By observing adults using these skills, children learn that even in difficult situations, it's possible to maintain respectful, open communication and work toward positive solutions.

For children with special needs, such as those with autism spectrum disorder (ASD) or ADHD, communication and conflict resolution may require additional support and tailored strategies. These children may struggle with reading social cues, understanding nonverbal communication, or managing their emotions during conflicts. Caregivers and educators should work closely with therapists or specialists to develop individualized approaches that meet the child's specific needs. For example, children with ASD might benefit from visual supports or social stories that help them understand different social situations and how to respond appropriately. In these cases, teaching communication and conflict resolution may require more repetition and structured practice, but with the right support, these children can still develop the skills they need to navigate social interactions successfully.

It's important to note that conflict resolution is a lifelong skill that continues to develop as children grow into adolescents and adults. The foundation laid in early childhood—through the consistent modeling and teaching of communication and conflict resolution skills—prepares children for the more complex conflicts they will face as they mature. Adolescents, in particular, may encounter new types of conflicts related to peer pressure, identity, or more significant interpersonal disputes. The skills they learned in childhood provide a crucial framework for handling these challenges in a constructive and emotionally healthy way.

For older children and teenagers, it's important to continue encouraging open communication and reinforcing conflict resolution strategies, while also respecting their growing independence. Adolescents may need more autonomy in resolving their conflicts, but caregivers should remain available to provide guidance and support when needed. This balance between independence and support helps teenagers feel confident in their ability to manage conflicts while knowing they have a trusted adult to turn to if they need help.

In summary, teaching communication and conflict resolution skills to children is an ongoing process that requires patience, modeling, and consistent practice. These skills not only help children navigate the social challenges of childhood but also lay the foundation for healthy, respectful relationships throughout their lives. By focusing on clear communication, empathy, and cooperative problem-solving, caregivers and educators can help children develop the tools they need to resolve conflicts peacefully and build strong, positive connections with others.e connections with others.

Handling ADHD and Autism

Handling children with ADHD (Attention Deficit Hyperactivity Disorder) and autism spectrum disorder (ASD) presents unique challenges, but also opportunities for growth and development when approached with understanding, patience, and targeted strategies. Both conditions involve distinct characteristics that affect a child's behavior, communication, and ability to function in social settings, and as such, caregivers and educators need to tailor their approaches to meet the individual needs of each child. Effective management of ADHD and autism involves not only addressing the behavioral symptoms but also nurturing the child's strengths and helping them develop the skills they need to navigate their environment successfully.

ADHD is a neurodevelopmental disorder characterized by persistent patterns of inattention, hyperactivity, and impulsivity that interfere with a child's daily functioning. Children with ADHD often struggle with tasks that require sustained focus, organization, and self-regulation. They may have difficulty sitting still, following instructions, completing tasks, or waiting their turn. These behaviors can sometimes be mistaken for laziness, defiance, or lack of discipline, but they are the result of underlying neurological differences that affect how the brain processes information.

Autism, or autism spectrum disorder (ASD), is a developmental disorder that affects social communication, behavior, and sensory processing. Children with autism may have difficulties understanding social cues, engaging in typical social interactions, or managing sensory input from their environment. They may exhibit repetitive behaviors, have restricted interests, or experience difficulty with changes in routine. The severity of autism varies widely, as it exists on a spectrum, meaning that some children may require significant support, while others may be able to function relatively independently.

In both ADHD and autism, the key to effective management is understanding that these are lifelong conditions that require ongoing support and accommodation. The goal is not to "cure" the child of their ADHD or autism, but to help them develop the skills they need to cope with challenges and succeed in their unique way. This requires a combination of strategies, including behavioral interventions, structured environments, clear communication, and, in some cases, medication or therapy.

Understanding ADHD: Key Characteristics and Challenges

Children with ADHD are often easily distracted, have trouble focusing, and may act impulsively without considering the consequences of their actions. They may struggle in environments that demand sustained attention, such as classrooms, or in situations that require them to wait patiently, follow multi-step instructions, or stay organized. Hyperactivity is also a common characteristic of ADHD, leading to behaviors such as fidgeting, excessive talking, or difficulty staying seated when expected to do so.

One of the most significant challenges for children with ADHD is regulating their attention. While they may appear inattentive or easily bored with tasks that require effort, they can also become intensely focused on activities they find particularly interesting—a phenomenon known as hyper focus. This inconsistency can be frustrating for caregivers and educators, as the child may seem capable of focusing in some situations but completely unfocused in others. Understanding that these fluctuations in attention are part of the ADHD profile is essential for providing appropriate support.

Another challenge is impulse control. Children with ADHD often act without thinking, which can lead to difficulties in social situations, such as interrupting conversations, grabbing items from others, or engaging in risky behaviors. These impulsive actions are not intentional misbehavior but are instead a reflection of the child's difficulty with self-regulation.

In terms of emotional regulation, children with ADHD may experience strong emotions, such as frustration, anger, or excitement, and may have difficulty managing these emotions in a way that is appropriate for the situation. This can result in emotional outbursts, mood swings, or feelings of overwhelm.

Strategies for Supporting Children with ADHD

One of the most effective ways to support children with ADHD is to provide a structured and predictable environment. Consistent routines help reduce the child's anxiety about what to expect and provide a sense of stability. For example, having a set schedule for meals, homework, playtime, and bedtime can help the child feel more in control and reduce impulsive or disruptive behavior.

Break tasks into smaller, manageable steps. Children with ADHD often become overwhelmed when faced with large or complex tasks, so breaking down activities into smaller steps can help them stay focused and complete the task. For example, instead of telling the child to "clean your room," it might be more effective to say, "First, pick up all the clothes on the floor, then put the toys in the toy bin." Providing visual checklists or written instructions can also help the child stay on track.

Clear, concise instructions are critical for children with ADHD. Because they may have difficulty processing long or complicated instructions, it's important to keep directions simple and direct. For instance, rather than saying, "I want you to clean your room, get dressed, and then come downstairs for breakfast," caregivers might give one instruction at a time: "First, clean your room."

Positive reinforcement can be a powerful tool in managing ADHD. Children with ADHD respond well to immediate feedback and rewards for good behavior. Rather than focusing on negative behaviors, caregivers can emphasize the positive by offering praise or small rewards when the child completes a task, follows instructions, or exhibits self-control. For example, using a sticker chart where the child earns a sticker for every completed task can be highly motivating, and once a certain number of stickers are earned, they can exchange them for a reward.

Physical activity is also essential for children with ADHD, as it helps them manage their energy levels and improve focus. Encouraging regular exercise, playtime, or movement breaks throughout the day can help reduce restlessness and hyperactivity, allowing the child to concentrate better when it's time for more structured activities. For instance, allowing the child to take a five-minute movement break between tasks can help them release excess energy and reset their focus.

In classroom settings, teachers can support children with ADHD by seating them in areas with fewer distractions, such as near the front of the room or away from windows. Providing fidget tools, such as stress balls or flexible seating options, can also help the child manage their need to move without being disruptive.

Understanding Autism: Key Characteristics and Challenges

Autism spectrum disorder (ASD) is a complex developmental condition that affects social communication, behavior, and sensory processing. Children with autism may have difficulty understanding social cues, such as facial expressions, tone of voice, or body language, which can make social interactions challenging. They may also struggle with understanding the "give and take" of conversations, leading to difficulties in making friends or engaging in typical social interactions.

Repetitive behaviors, such as hand-flapping, rocking, or repeating phrases, are common among children with autism. These behaviors, known as "stimming," are often used by the child as a way to self-regulate and cope with sensory overload or emotional stress. While these behaviors may seem unusual to others, they serve an important function for the child and should not be discouraged unless they are harmful or disruptive.

Children with autism often have strong preferences for routine and structure and may become distressed by changes in their environment or schedule. For example, a sudden change in plans, such as an unexpected trip to the grocery store, might lead to a meltdown. Sensory sensitivities are also common in children with autism, with some children being highly sensitive to noise, lights, textures, or smells. These sensory sensitivities can lead to sensory overload, which can trigger anxiety, meltdowns, or withdrawal.

Another hallmark of autism is restricted interests, where the child may have an intense focus on specific topics or activities. These interests can provide a source of joy and comfort for the child but may also limit their willingness to engage in other activities or social interactions.

Strategies for Supporting Children with Autism

Supporting children with autism requires a deep understanding of their individual needs, preferences, and communication styles. Because autism exists on a spectrum, no two children with autism will have the same challenges or strengths, so it's important to tailor strategies to each child's unique profile.

Structured environments and routines are essential for children with autism. These children often thrive in predictable settings where they know what to expect and can rely on familiar routines. Visual schedules, which use pictures or symbols to represent different parts of the day, can help the child understand and anticipate transitions between activities. For example, a visual schedule might show a picture of a bed to represent bedtime, followed by a picture of a toothbrush to represent brushing teeth. These visual cues can reduce anxiety and help the child navigate their day with greater independence.

Social stories are another effective tool for teaching social skills and preparing children for new or challenging situations. A social story is a short, simple narrative that describes a situation, along with appropriate responses and behaviors. For example, a social story might explain what to expect at a doctor's appointment and how to respond when the doctor asks questions. By reading social stories in advance, children with autism can rehearse social interactions and feel more confident in navigating them.

For children with sensory sensitivities, creating a sensory-friendly environment is crucial. This might involve minimizing loud noises, providing noise-canceling headphones, using soft lighting, or allowing the child to wear clothing that feels comfortable to them. In situations where sensory overload is likely, such as crowded places or noisy events, providing a "sensory break" can help the child regulate their emotions and avoid meltdowns. A sensory break might involve allowing the child to retreat to a quiet room, engage in calming activities such as deep breathing or squeezing a stress ball, or use sensory tools like weighted blankets.

Communication support is often necessary for children with autism, particularly those who are nonverbal or have limited verbal communication. Augmentative and alternative communication (AAC) tools, such as picture exchange communication systems (PECS) or speech-generating devices, can help children express their needs and feelings. These tools allow the child to use pictures, symbols, or technology to communicate, which can reduce frustration and improve their ability to engage with others.

Supporting social skills development is another important aspect of working with children with autism. Social skills training, either through one-on-one sessions with a therapist or in a group setting, can help the child with autism learn how to engage with peers, understand social cues, and navigate typical social interactions. This training can involve role-playing different social scenarios, teaching the child how to initiate conversations, and helping them recognize nonverbal communication, such as facial expressions or body language. Social skills groups, often led by a therapist, provide children with autism an opportunity to practice these skills in a structured, supportive environment alongside peers who may be working on similar goals.

It's also important to recognize and nurture the child's interests and strengths, even if those interests may seem narrow or repetitive. For example, if a child with autism has a deep interest in trains, caregivers and educators can use that interest as a way to build social skills, academic learning, or communication abilities. This might involve encouraging the child to share facts about trains with others or using train-themed activities to teach math, reading, or problem-solving skills. By leveraging the child's natural interests, caregivers can create positive learning experiences that feel meaningful and engaging for the child.

For children with autism who exhibit repetitive behaviors, it's essential to understand that these behaviors often serve as a coping mechanism for dealing with stress or sensory overload. While it may be tempting to discourage these behaviors, it's important to recognize that they provide comfort and help the child self-regulate. Rather than trying to eliminate repetitive behaviors entirely, caregivers should focus on creating an environment where the child feels safe and supported, while also teaching alternative coping strategies if the behavior becomes disruptive or harmful.

For example, if a child flaps their hands when they are feeling anxious, caregivers might offer them a stress ball to squeeze or encourage them to take deep breaths as an alternative way to manage their anxiety. Over time, the child can learn to use these alternative strategies in addition to their existing coping mechanisms, giving them more tools to handle stressful situations.

Managing Emotional and Behavioral Challenges in ADHD and Autism

Both children with ADHD and autism may experience emotional and behavioral challenges, such as meltdowns, tantrums, or outbursts, when they become overwhelmed or frustrated. These behaviors can be particularly challenging for caregivers to manage, but they are often a sign that the child is struggling to cope with their emotions or sensory environment. Understanding the root causes of these behaviors is key to managing them effectively.

Meltdowns in children with autism are often triggered by sensory overload, changes in routine, or overwhelming emotions. A meltdown is different from a tantrum, in that it is not a goal-oriented behavior (such as seeking attention or trying to get something), but rather an intense emotional response to overwhelming stimuli. During a meltdown, the child may become physically agitated, scream, cry, or engage in self-soothing behaviors like rocking or covering their ears.

To manage meltdowns, caregivers should focus on creating a calm, quiet environment where the child can self-regulate. Removing the child from the overwhelming situation, providing sensory tools like noise-canceling headphones, or guiding the child through calming activities like deep breathing or squeezing a sensory toy can help de-escalate the situation. It's also important to avoid trying to reason with or discipline the child during a meltdown, as they are likely unable to process verbal instructions or consequences in the moment. Instead, focus on helping the child regain a sense of calm before addressing the situation.

Tantrums, which are more common in children with ADHD, often occur when the child is frustrated, tired, or seeking attention. While tantrums may involve similar behaviors to meltdowns—such as crying, yelling, or throwing objects—the key difference is that tantrums are typically goal-directed. For example, a child might throw a tantrum because they want a toy or because they are upset about having to stop an activity they enjoy.

Managing tantrums in children with ADHD requires a combination of clear boundaries and emotional regulation strategies. Caregivers should establish consistent expectations and consequences for tantrum behaviors, while also providing support to help the child manage their emotions. For example, if a child throws a tantrum because they don't want to do their homework, the caregiver might calmly acknowledge the child's feelings—"I know you're frustrated that you have to stop playing to do homework"—while reinforcing the expectation that homework still needs to be completed. Providing positive reinforcement for calm behavior and offering breaks or rewards for completing tasks can also help reduce the frequency of tantrums over time.

For both ADHD and autism, emotional regulation skills are crucial for managing behavioral challenges. Teaching children how to recognize their emotions, express them appropriately, and use coping strategies to manage intense feelings can significantly reduce the likelihood of meltdowns or tantrums. Caregivers can support this process by modeling emotional regulation in their own behavior, offering praise and encouragement when the child uses coping strategies, and providing structured opportunities for the child to practice these skills.

Collaborating with Therapists and Educators

Collaboration between caregivers, educators, and therapists is essential for supporting children with ADHD and autism. Because both conditions require ongoing, individualized support, it's important for all members of the child's care team to be aligned in their approach to managing behavior, teaching skills, and providing accommodations.

For children with ADHD, educators can play a critical role in creating a classroom environment that supports their learning needs. This might involve providing accommodations such as extended time for tests, frequent breaks, or allowing the child to use fidget tools to help them focus. Teachers can also work with caregivers to develop behavior plans that use positive reinforcement to encourage desired behaviors, such as staying on task or following instructions.

For children with autism, educators may need to provide additional supports, such as visual schedules, social stories, or sensory breaks throughout the day. Collaboration with speech therapists, occupational therapists, or special education teachers may also be necessary to support the child's communication and sensory needs in the classroom. By working together, caregivers, educators, and therapists can create a cohesive support system that helps the child succeed both academically and socially.

In addition to school-based supports, children with ADHD and autism may benefit from therapeutic interventions such as cognitive-behavioral therapy (CBT), social skills training, or occupational therapy. CBT can be particularly helpful for children with ADHD, as it focuses on teaching them how to manage their attention, regulate their emotions, and develop problem-solving skills. Social skills training, as mentioned earlier, is often a key component of therapy for children with autism, helping them learn how to navigate social interactions and build relationships with peers.

For children with sensory processing challenges, occupational therapy can provide valuable tools and strategies for managing sensory input. Occupational therapists can work with the child to develop sensory diets—customized plans that include activities and tools designed to help the child regulate their sensory needs. For example, a sensory diet might include activities like jumping on a trampoline, swinging, or using weighted blankets to help the child feel more grounded and focused.

Medication may also be part of the treatment plan for children with ADHD. Stimulant medications, such as methylphenidate (Ritalin) or amphetamines (Adderall), are commonly prescribed to help children with ADHD manage their attention and impulse control. While medication is not a cure for ADHD, it can be a helpful tool for reducing symptoms and improving the child's ability to function in daily life. Caregivers should work closely with the child's doctor to monitor the effectiveness of the medication and adjust dosages as needed.

For children with autism, medication is typically not the first line of treatment, but it may be used to manage specific symptoms such as anxiety, aggression, or hyperactivity. Caregivers should discuss any concerns about medication with the child's healthcare provider and weigh the potential benefits and risks before making a decision.

Creating a Supportive Home Environment

At home, caregivers can create an environment that supports the unique needs of children with ADHD and autism by providing structure, consistency, and opportunities for growth. For children with ADHD, a structured routine that includes regular breaks, clear expectations, and positive reinforcement can help reduce impulsive behavior and improve focus. Providing a quiet, organized space for homework or quiet activities can also minimize distractions and help the child concentrate.

For children with autism, creating a sensory-friendly environment is crucial. This might involve setting up a designated sensory space where the child can go to calm down when they feel overwhelmed, using dim lighting or soft textures, and minimizing loud or sudden noises. Caregivers should also be mindful of the child's need for routine and predictability, offering clear communication about any changes in plans or expectations.

In both cases, it's important for caregivers to be patient, empathetic, and supportive. Children with ADHD and autism may take longer to develop certain skills, and they may need more time and practice to navigate social interactions, complete tasks, or manage their emotions. Caregivers should celebrate small victories, provide encouragement, and recognize the child's unique strengths and abilities.

In conclusion, handling ADHD and autism requires a comprehensive approach that addresses the child's individual needs, supports their development, and fosters their strengths. By providing structure, clear communication, positive reinforcement, and access to specialized therapies, caregivers and educators can help children with ADHD and autism thrive in both social and academic settings. Through collaboration, patience, and understanding, these children can learn to manage their challenges and build the skills they need for a successful and fulfilling life.

Addressing Trauma-Related Behaviors

Addressing trauma-related behaviors in children requires a nuanced and compassionate approach, as trauma affects a child's emotional, psychological, and behavioral development in profound ways. Children who have experienced trauma—whether from abuse, neglect, violence, the loss of a loved one, or other significant stressors—often struggle to process their emotions and may exhibit challenging behaviors as a result. These behaviors are not signs of bad character or deliberate defiance, but rather survival responses to overwhelming experiences. Understanding the root causes of trauma-related behaviors and providing a supportive environment where children can heal is crucial for helping them regain a sense of safety and emotional stability.

Trauma can manifest in various ways, depending on the child's age, personality, the nature of the traumatic event, and the level of support they have received. Some common behaviors associated with trauma include aggression, withdrawal, emotional dysregulation, hypervigilance, and difficulty trusting others. These behaviors are often defense mechanisms that the child has developed to protect themselves in response to danger or stress. While these behaviors may have served a purpose during the traumatic event, they can become maladaptive in everyday life, interfering with the child's ability to form relationships, focus in school, or engage in typical childhood activities.

At the core of trauma-related behaviors is the child's need to feel safe. Trauma disrupts a child's sense of security and trust, leading to feelings of fear, helplessness, and unpredictability. Children who have experienced trauma may have difficulty distinguishing between safe and unsafe situations, which can lead to hypervigilance—a heightened state of alertness where the child is constantly on guard for potential threats. This hypervigilance can make it difficult for the child to relax, concentrate, or engage in normal activities, as they are always scanning their environment for danger. In some cases, children may overreact to minor stressors or perceive threats where none exist, resulting in behaviors that seem disproportionate to the situation.

One of the most common trauma-related behaviors is emotional dysregulation, where the child struggles to manage and express their emotions in a healthy way. Children who have experienced trauma may have intense mood swings, frequent meltdowns, or difficulty calming down after becoming upset. These emotional outbursts can be triggered by seemingly small events, as the child's nervous system is often in a heightened state of arousal due to their trauma. For example, a child who has experienced abuse might become extremely distressed if an adult raises their voice, even if the adult is not angry or threatening. This emotional sensitivity can make it difficult for the child to regulate their reactions and respond to stress in a constructive way.

Aggression is another common behavior in children who have experienced trauma, particularly if the trauma involved violence or abuse. Children who have learned that the world is unsafe may become aggressive as a way to protect themselves from perceived threats. They may lash out physically or verbally when they feel cornered, afraid, or overwhelmed. In some cases, the child may not even be aware of the underlying emotions driving their aggression, as they have become so accustomed to responding to stress with fight-or-flight behaviors.

Withdrawal and avoidance are other trauma-related behaviors that children may exhibit. Some children respond to trauma by shutting down emotionally and socially, withdrawing from relationships, and avoiding situations that remind them of the trauma. They may seem detached, unresponsive, or disinterested in activities they once enjoyed. This emotional numbness is often a defense mechanism that the child uses to avoid being overwhelmed by feelings of fear, sadness, or helplessness. However, this withdrawal can lead to further isolation and difficulty building trust with others, making it harder for the child to develop healthy relationships.

Another behavior often seen in traumatized children is reenactment, where the child relives aspects of the trauma through play, dreams, or repetitive behaviors. This may include acting out the trauma in their interactions with others, engaging in risky behaviors, or playing out violent or distressing scenarios with toys or during imaginative play. Reenactment can be a way for the child to process their trauma, but it can also be distressing for both the child and those around them, particularly if the child is unable to break free from the cycle of reliving the traumatic event.

Given the complexity of trauma-related behaviors, it is essential for caregivers and educators to approach these children with empathy and understanding, recognizing that the behaviors are a response to pain and fear rather than willful disobedience or defiance. The first step in addressing trauma-related behaviors is creating a safe and predictable environment where the child can begin to heal. Safety is the foundation of any trauma-informed approach, as children who have experienced trauma often feel that their world is chaotic and unpredictable. Providing consistency, clear boundaries, and a calm atmosphere helps the child regain a sense of control and security.

Caregivers and educators should also be aware of potential triggers that may cause the child to relive the trauma or respond with heightened emotions. These triggers can vary widely depending on the child's trauma, but they often include loud noises, sudden movements, certain smells, or specific locations that remind the child of the traumatic event. Understanding these triggers and helping the child avoid or manage them is crucial for reducing trauma-related behaviors. For example, if a child becomes anxious in crowded or noisy environments, caregivers might create a quiet space where the child can retreat when they feel overwhelmed. Similarly, if a certain activity or situation reminds the child of their trauma, caregivers can provide alternative activities or support the child through the experience with patience and reassurance.

One of the most effective ways to help children with trauma-related behaviors is to teach emotional regulation skills. Children who have experienced trauma often struggle to identify and manage their emotions, leading to frequent meltdowns or outbursts. Caregivers can support these children by helping them develop a vocabulary for their emotions and teaching them strategies for calming down when they feel overwhelmed. For example, deep breathing exercises, progressive muscle relaxation, or using a calming sensory tool like a stress ball can help the child regain control over their emotions during moments of distress. Over time, as the child practices these techniques, they may become better able to self-regulate and manage their emotional responses without relying on external interventions.

It is also important to model emotional regulation for children who have experienced trauma. Children often learn how to manage their emotions by watching the adults around them, so caregivers and educators should strive to remain calm and composed, even in challenging situations. For example, if a child has an emotional outburst, the caregiver might model calm behavior by taking deep breaths and speaking in a soothing tone, demonstrating to the child that it is possible to manage intense emotions without escalating the situation. This not only helps the child feel safer but also provides them with a concrete example of how to handle difficult feelings in a healthy way.

Positive reinforcement can be an effective tool for encouraging desired behaviors in children with trauma-related issues. Trauma can erode a child's self-esteem and sense of worth, so offering praise and rewards for positive behaviors helps rebuild their confidence and reinforces the idea that they are capable of making good choices. Caregivers should be specific in their praise, focusing on the behavior they want to encourage rather than giving general compliments. For example, instead of saying, "Good job," a caregiver might say, "I'm really proud of how you used your words to tell me you were upset instead of hitting." This reinforces the specific behavior the caregiver wants to see more of and helps the child understand what they did well.

For children with trauma-related behaviors, it's also important to provide opportunities for connection and trust-building. Trauma can cause children to become distrustful of others, particularly adults, so creating a strong, supportive relationship with the child is key to helping them heal. This can be achieved through consistent, caring interactions that show the child they are valued and understood. Caregivers should make time to engage with the child in activities they enjoy, offer physical comfort when appropriate, and listen actively when the child wants to talk about their feelings or experiences. Over time, these interactions help the child rebuild their sense of trust in others, which is a critical step in the healing process.

Therapeutic interventions are often necessary for children who have experienced significant trauma, particularly if their trauma-related behaviors are severe or persistent. Trauma-focused cognitive behavioral therapy (TF-CBT) is one of the most effective therapeutic approaches for helping children process and recover from trauma. TF-CBT combines cognitive behavioral techniques with trauma-informed practices to help the child process their traumatic experiences, develop healthy coping mechanisms, and improve emotional regulation. In TF-CBT, the therapist works with both the child and their caregivers to address the child's symptoms and provide a safe space for healing.

Play therapy is another therapeutic approach that can be particularly beneficial for young children who have experienced trauma. In play therapy, the child is encouraged to express their feelings and experiences through play, which allows them to process their trauma in a way that feels safe and manageable. The therapist uses the child's play as a window into their emotions, helping the child work through difficult feelings and behaviors in a supportive environment. For children who have difficulty expressing their emotions verbally, play therapy provides an alternative outlet for processing their trauma.

Art therapy and other creative therapies can also be helpful for children who have experienced trauma. These therapies allow the child to express their feelings through artistic mediums, such as drawing, painting, or music, which can be less intimidating than talking about their trauma directly. Creative therapies help the child process their emotions in a non-verbal way, making it easier for them to access and express difficult feelings.

For caregivers and educators working with children who have experienced trauma, self-care is an essential part of the process. Supporting a traumatized child can be emotionally taxing, and caregivers may experience secondary trauma as a result of their work. It's important for caregivers to seek support when needed, whether through professional counseling, peer support groups, or regular self-care practices. By taking care of their own emotional needs, caregivers can be more present and effective in supporting the child's healing journey.

Creating a trauma-informed environment is essential for addressing trauma-related behaviors in children. A trauma-informed environment is one in which all aspects of care, education, and support are designed with an understanding of the effects of trauma and a commitment to fostering safety, empowerment, and healing. This approach recognizes that behaviors that may seem disruptive or challenging are often the result of underlying trauma, and that addressing the child's emotional needs is critical to helping them succeed.

A key aspect of creating a trauma-informed environment is providing predictable routines and clear expectations. Trauma can make children feel that the world is unpredictable and unsafe, so establishing a daily routine that the child can rely on helps them regain a sense of control. Routines should be communicated clearly and consistently, so the child knows what to expect throughout the day. For example, in a classroom setting, a visual schedule can help children anticipate transitions and feel more secure, while at home, a predictable bedtime routine can provide a sense of comfort and stability.

Consistency in responses to behavior is also important in a trauma-informed environment. Children who have experienced trauma may struggle with trusting adults, especially if their trauma involved inconsistent or unpredictable care giving. It's important for caregivers and educators to respond to the child's behaviors in a calm and predictable way, even when the child is acting out. This consistency helps the child understand that they are safe and that the adults in their life can be relied upon to provide support and guidance, no matter what.

One of the principles of trauma-informed care is avoiding re-traumatization. Re-traumatization occurs when a child is exposed to situations or interactions that remind them of their original trauma, causing them to relive those feelings of fear, helplessness, or danger. Caregivers and educators must be mindful of how certain practices or environments might inadvertently trigger the child's trauma. For example, harsh discipline, yelling, or physical restraint can trigger a child who has experienced abuse or violence. Instead, trauma-informed practices emphasize the use of gentle, supportive interventions that prioritize the child's emotional well-being.

Another important aspect of trauma-informed care is empowering the child to have a sense of control over their environment. Trauma often strips children of their sense of agency, leaving them feeling powerless and out of control. By providing opportunities for the child to make choices and have a say in their daily activities, caregivers help the child regain a sense of empowerment. For example, allowing the child to choose what game to play, what book to read, or what snack to have can give them a sense of control over their environment and reduce feelings of helplessness.

Caregivers and educators should also focus on building resilience in children who have experienced trauma. Resilience is the ability to bounce back from adversity, and it can be nurtured through supportive relationships, positive self-esteem, and the development of coping skills. Helping children build resilience involves providing them with opportunities to succeed, offering praise for their efforts, and teaching them how to manage stress and setbacks in a healthy way. Over time, these experiences help the child develop the inner strength to cope with challenges and move forward in their healing process.

In addition to direct support for the child, involving the family in the healing process is crucial. Family dynamics often play a significant role in a child's trauma and recovery, so it's important to work with the child's caregivers to create a supportive home environment. Trauma-focused family therapy can help address any family issues that may be contributing to the child's behavior, while also teaching caregivers how to support the child's emotional needs. This collaborative approach ensures that the child is receiving consistent care and support across all environments, which is essential for their long-term healing.

It's also important to recognize that trauma can have lasting effects on a child's brain development. Research shows that early trauma can alter the structure and function of the brain, particularly in areas related to stress regulation, emotional control, and memory. This means that children who have experienced trauma may need additional support in areas like attention, memory, and executive functioning. Caregivers and educators can help by providing accommodations, such as extra time to complete tasks, step-by-step instructions, or sensory breaks to help the child stay focused and calm.

For children who have experienced trauma, building healthy relationships is a key part of the healing process. Relationships provide the foundation for emotional healing, as they help the child learn to trust others and feel valued. Caregivers and educators can support this process by consistently offering warmth, empathy, and understanding, even when the child's behaviors are challenging. These relationships help the child rebuild their sense of self-worth and begin to see the world as a safer, more predictable place.

In some cases, children who have experienced trauma may also struggle with attachment issues, particularly if their trauma involved neglect or disruptions in care giving. These children may have difficulty forming close relationships or may exhibit anxious, avoidant, or disorganized attachment behaviors. Addressing attachment issues often requires specialized therapeutic interventions, such as attachment-based therapy, which focuses on rebuilding trust and fostering secure, healthy relationships. This type of therapy helps the child develop a stronger emotional bond with caregivers, which is critical for their overall emotional development and well-being.

It's essential for caregivers to recognize the signs of secondary trauma or burnout in themselves, especially when working with children who have experienced significant trauma. Supporting a child with trauma-related behaviors can be emotionally draining, and caregivers may experience feelings of helplessness, frustration, or emotional exhaustion. Caregivers need to prioritize their own mental health by seeking support from colleagues, supervisors, or therapists, and by engaging in regular self-care practices. This allows them to remain emotionally available and effective in their role, providing the child with the consistent support they need.

Schools play a critical role in supporting children with trauma-related behaviors, as many children spend a significant portion of their day in the school environment. Trauma-informed educational practices emphasize creating a safe and supportive learning environment, where students feel valued and understood. Teachers can support students with trauma by using positive reinforcement, offering accommodations for emotional or behavioral challenges, and creating opportunities for the child to succeed academically and socially. Building strong relationships between teachers and students is essential for helping traumatized children feel safe and supported in the classroom.

Additionally, schools can implement trauma-informed policies that provide staff with training on how to recognize and respond to trauma-related behaviors. This training helps educators understand the impact of trauma on learning and behavior, and equips them with strategies for supporting students in a compassionate and effective way. By adopting a trauma-informed approach, schools can create an environment where all students, including those with trauma histories, have the opportunity to thrive.

In conclusion, addressing trauma-related behaviors in children requires a comprehensive, trauma-informed approach that prioritizes safety, emotional regulation, and relationship-building. By understanding the root causes of trauma-related behaviors and providing a supportive, predictable environment, caregivers and educators can help children regain a sense of control and begin the healing process. With patience, empathy, and appropriate therapeutic interventions, children who have experienced trauma can develop the resilience and skills they need to overcome their challenges and lead fulfilling, healthy lives.

Sibling Rivalry and School Conflicts

Sibling rivalry and school conflicts are common issues in the social and emotional development of children. These conflicts, whether between siblings at home or peers at school, are often rooted in competition for attention, resources, or status. While sibling rivalry and peer conflicts can be frustrating for caregivers and educators, they are also opportunities for children to learn valuable life skills, such as problem-solving, emotional regulation, empathy, and effective communication.

Addressing sibling rivalry and school conflicts requires a balanced approach that acknowledges the normalcy of conflict while providing children with tools to manage disagreements in a constructive way. Both scenarios—rivalry between siblings and conflicts with school peers—require the development of healthy conflict resolution strategies that not only resolve the immediate disagreement but also foster long-term skills for managing relationships and emotions.

Understanding Sibling Rivalry

Sibling rivalry is a natural part of growing up in a family with more than one child. Siblings often compete for parental attention, approval, and resources, such as toys, space, and privileges. Rivalry can manifest in various ways, including verbal arguments, physical fights, jealousy, and attempts to outshine one another. While sibling rivalry is normal, it can become problematic if it leads to persistent conflict, resentment, or feelings of inadequacy in one or more children.

Sibling rivalry often intensifies during significant transitions in family dynamics, such as the birth of a new sibling, parental separation or divorce, or changes in living arrangements. These transitions can exacerbate feelings of insecurity or jealousy, leading to an increase in rivalry behaviors. For example, an older child may become resentful when a new baby is born, feeling that their parents' attention has shifted away from them. Similarly, a child who feels overshadowed by a sibling's academic or athletic achievements may become more competitive or withdrawn.

One of the key factors that fuel sibling rivalry is the perceived favoritism by parents. Children are highly attuned to how their parents treat them in comparison to their siblings, and even subtle differences in treatment can lead to feelings of unfairness. While it's nearly impossible for parents to treat each child exactly the same, it's important for parents to be mindful of how their actions and words might be interpreted by their children. Children need to feel that they are valued for their unique qualities, and that their parents' love and attention are not conditional on their performance or behavior in comparison to their siblings.

Strategies for Managing Sibling Rivalry

One of the most effective strategies for managing sibling rivalry is to teach children how to express their feelings and needs in constructive ways. Often, rivalry stems from feelings of frustration, jealousy, or insecurity that the child doesn't know how to articulate. By helping children develop a vocabulary for their emotions, parents can prevent minor disagreements from escalating into full-blown fights. For example, if one child feels that their sibling is always being praised for good grades, the parent might encourage the child to express their feelings by saying, "I feel sad when I don't get as much praise as my brother for doing well in school."

It's also important for parents to avoid comparing their children to one another, as this can fuel rivalry and resentment. Statements like "Why can't you be more like your sister?" or "Your brother never behaves like this" send the message that one child is better or more valued than the other, which can damage the child's self-esteem and exacerbate competition between siblings. Instead, parents should focus on praising each child for their individual strengths and accomplishments, without making comparisons. For example, a parent might say, "I'm proud of how hard you worked on your project," rather than comparing the child's work to their sibling's.

Another effective approach is to encourage cooperation rather than competition between siblings. Parents can do this by creating opportunities for siblings to work together on shared tasks or activities, such as cooking a meal, playing a game, or completing a household chore. By fostering a sense of teamwork, parents can help their children see their siblings as allies rather than rivals. Offering praise for cooperative behavior, such as sharing or taking turns, reinforces the idea that working together benefits everyone.

Setting clear and consistent rules for behavior is also important in managing sibling rivalry. Sibling conflicts often arise when one child feels that their sibling is being unfair or breaking the rules. By establishing clear boundaries and consequences for aggressive or disrespectful behavior, parents can create a sense of fairness and accountability. For example, a family rule might be that hitting or name-calling is never allowed, and that any disputes must be resolved through calm communication or by seeking help from an adult. When rules are consistently enforced, children are less likely to engage in destructive behaviors, as they know there will be consequences.

It's important to acknowledge that siblings won't always get along perfectly, and that occasional conflicts are inevitable. However, rather than stepping in to resolve every argument, parents should encourage their children to develop their own conflict-resolution skills. This might involve teaching children how to negotiate, compromise, or take turns. For example, if two siblings are arguing over a toy, the parent might ask them to come up with a solution together, such as taking turns playing with the toy for a set amount of time. By giving children the opportunity to resolve their own conflicts, parents help them develop important social skills that will serve them well in other areas of life.

In situations where sibling rivalry becomes intense or persistent, family therapy may be helpful in addressing underlying issues. A family therapist can work with the family to improve communication, identify the root causes of rivalry, and develop strategies for managing conflict in a healthy way. Therapy can also provide a safe space for siblings to express their feelings and work through any resentment or jealousy they may be experiencing.

Understanding School Conflicts

School conflicts are another common challenge for children as they navigate the social dynamics of the classroom and playground. Conflicts with peers can arise over a wide range of issues, including disagreements over games, competition for popularity, bullying, or misunderstandings. Just like sibling rivalry, school conflicts provide an opportunity for children to develop conflict-resolution skills, but they can also be a source of stress, anxiety, and social isolation if not addressed properly.

One of the most common types of school conflicts involves disputes over games or activities during recess or free time. Children may argue over the rules of a game, who gets to participate, or who is "in charge." These conflicts often arise because children are still learning how to negotiate, share, and take turns. While these disagreements are a normal part of social development, they can escalate if not handled constructively.

Another common source of school conflict is bullying, which involves repeated aggressive behavior aimed at hurting or intimidating another child. Bullying can take many forms, including physical aggression, verbal insults, social exclusion, or online harassment (cyberbullying). Unlike typical conflicts, bullying is characterized by a power imbalance, where one child uses their strength, popularity, or social influence to dominate or control another child. Bullying can have serious emotional and psychological consequences for the victim, leading to anxiety, depression, and a loss of self-esteem.

Friendship conflicts are another challenge that many children face in school. As children form and navigate friendships, they may experience conflicts over issues such as jealousy, exclusion, or misunderstandings. For example, one child may feel hurt if their friend chooses to play with someone else, leading to feelings of rejection or betrayal. These conflicts are often fueled by the intense emotions that children feel about their friendships, and they may have difficulty expressing or managing these emotions in a constructive way.

Strategies for Managing School Conflicts

Teaching children how to resolve school conflicts is an important part of their social development. One of the most effective strategies for managing school conflicts is teaching children communication skills, including how to express their feelings, listen to others, and negotiate solutions. Caregivers and educators can help children practice these skills by role-playing common conflict scenarios and guiding them through the process of resolving the conflict peacefully.

For example, if two children are arguing over a game during recess, the teacher might help them express their feelings by saying, "It sounds like you're both upset because you want to play the game your way. Can we come up with a solution where everyone gets a turn?" This approach encourages the children to articulate their needs while also working together to find a compromise. Over time, children can learn to use these communication skills independently to resolve their own conflicts without adult intervention.

Conflict resolution skills should also include teaching children how to manage their emotions during disagreements. Children who feel angry, frustrated, or hurt during a conflict may struggle to think clearly or communicate effectively, leading to escalation. Teaching children calming strategies, such as deep breathing, counting to ten, or taking a break from the situation, can help them regain control of their emotions before attempting to resolve the conflict.

For children involved in bullying, it's important to address the issue promptly and directly. Schools should have clear anti-bullying policies in place, and caregivers and educators should work together to ensure that these policies are enforced consistently. Victims of bullying need support to help them rebuild their self-esteem and feel safe at school. This might involve providing the child with a trusted adult they can talk to, offering counseling, or helping them build new friendships.

For the child engaging in bullying behavior, it's important to understand the underlying reasons for their actions. Often, children who bully others are dealing with their own emotional issues, such as low self-esteem, insecurity, or problems at home. Addressing these root causes through counseling or behavioral interventions can help the child develop healthier ways of interacting with their peers.

Encouraging empathy and perspective-taking is another important strategy for managing school conflicts. Children often get caught up in their own emotions and may have difficulty seeing things from the other person's point of view. Teaching children to consider how their actions affect others, and helping them understand the feelings and perspectives of their peers, can reduce conflict and foster more positive relationships. For example, a teacher might say, "How do you think your friend felt when you wouldn't let them play? What could you do to make things right?"

Teachers can also create a positive classroom environment that emphasizes respect, inclusivity, and collaboration. By fostering a culture of kindness and support, teachers can help prevent conflicts from arising in the first place. Activities that promote teamwork and cooperation, such as group projects or team-building exercises, can enhance students' social skills and help them learn to navigate conflicts more effectively. Additionally, incorporating social-emotional learning (SEL) programs into the curriculum can provide students with the tools they need to understand and manage their emotions, develop empathy, and build healthy relationships.

Conflict resolution can also be taught through structured programs or workshops that focus on specific skills, such as negotiation, communication, and problem-solving. These programs often include role-playing, discussions, and activities that help children practice their skills in a supportive environment. For example, a school might implement a peer mediation program where trained students facilitate discussions between their peers to help resolve conflicts. This not only empowers students but also reinforces the importance of collaboration and mutual respect.

When conflicts do arise, it's essential for both caregivers and educators to approach the situation with a calm and objective mindset. Instead of assigning blame or taking sides, adults should act as facilitators, guiding the children through the process of resolving their conflict. This approach not only helps the children learn effective problem-solving skills but also reinforces the idea that conflicts can be resolved without aggression or hostility.

In situations where conflicts escalate or involve serious bullying behaviors, it's important to intervene immediately and take appropriate action. This may involve separating the children involved, gathering information about what happened, and ensuring the safety of all students. School policies should provide clear guidelines on how to handle such situations, including reporting procedures and consequences for bullying behavior. Adults should work to address the root causes of the conflict and provide appropriate support for all children involved.

Additionally, schools should create an environment that encourages open communication about conflicts and bullying. This can involve establishing anonymous reporting systems, regular check-ins with students about their social experiences, and promoting a culture where students feel safe to speak up about their concerns. Providing training for staff on how to recognize and respond to bullying behaviors can also enhance the school's ability to address conflicts effectively.

Parental involvement is crucial in managing sibling rivalry and school conflicts. Parents can support their children by encouraging open communication about their feelings and experiences. By creating a safe space for children to share their thoughts, parents can help them process their emotions and develop better conflict resolution skills. Parents should also model healthy communication and conflict resolution strategies in their interactions with their children and each other. Children learn by example, so demonstrating respectful communication, active listening, and effective problem-solving can reinforce these skills in children.

In situations where siblings are involved in conflict, parents can facilitate discussions between the siblings to help them express their feelings and needs. For example, parents can encourage siblings to use "I" statements to communicate their feelings and guide them toward finding common ground. By helping siblings practice these skills, parents can reduce rivalries and promote a more harmonious family dynamic.

Parents should also be mindful of how they discuss conflicts at home. Avoiding negative comparisons between siblings and reinforcing each child's unique strengths and qualities can help reduce feelings of competition and jealousy. When addressing conflicts, parents should emphasize teamwork and cooperation, reminding siblings that they are on the same team and can work together to solve problems.

While sibling rivalry and school conflicts can be challenging, they also present valuable opportunities for growth and learning. By fostering effective communication, empathy, and conflict resolution skills, caregivers and educators can help children navigate these conflicts in a constructive way. Children who learn to manage conflicts effectively are better equipped to build positive relationships, work collaboratively, and navigate the complexities of social interactions throughout their lives.

Furthermore, it is essential to recognize that the experiences children have with conflict in childhood can shape their future relationships. By teaching children healthy conflict resolution strategies and providing support during challenging situations, caregivers and educators can help children develop a toolkit of skills that will serve them well into adulthood. These skills include effective communication, emotional regulation, empathy, and the ability to negotiate and compromise—all of which are critical for maintaining healthy relationships.

In conclusion, sibling rivalry and school conflicts are normal aspects of childhood development that can provide opportunities for learning and growth. Addressing these conflicts requires a thoughtful and supportive approach that prioritizes effective communication, emotional regulation, and the development of conflict resolution skills. By creating a safe and nurturing environment, caregivers and educators can help children navigate these challenges and build strong, positive relationships with their siblings and peers. Through patience, empathy, and a commitment to teaching essential skills, adults can guide children toward becoming confident, resilient individuals who can successfully manage conflicts throughout their lives.

Building Emotional Intelligence

Building emotional intelligence in children is a vital long-term strategy that supports their social, emotional, and academic development. Emotional intelligence (EI) refers to the ability to recognize, understand, and manage one's own emotions while also being able to recognize, understand, and influence the emotions of others. Research has shown that high emotional intelligence contributes to better mental health, stronger relationships, and improved academic performance. Therefore, fostering emotional intelligence from a young age equips children with the tools they need to navigate the complexities of life and establish meaningful connections with others.

Emotional intelligence consists of several key components, including self-awareness, self-regulation, social awareness, and relationship management. Each of these components plays a crucial role in a child's ability to understand their own feelings, cope with challenges, empathize with others, and build healthy relationships. By focusing on these elements, caregivers and educators can create an environment that nurtures emotional growth and resilience.

One of the foundational aspects of emotional intelligence is self-awareness. Self-awareness involves recognizing one's emotions, understanding the triggers that cause certain feelings, and being able to accurately assess one's strengths and weaknesses. For children, developing self-awareness begins with emotional vocabulary—learning to identify and label their feelings.

Caregivers can support this development by openly discussing emotions in everyday situations and encouraging children to articulate how they feel.

Using age-appropriate language, caregivers can model emotional vocabulary in conversations with their children. For example, when a child seems upset after losing a game, the caregiver might say, "It's okay to feel sad when things don't go your way. You worked hard, and it's natural to feel disappointed." By naming emotions and discussing their causes, caregivers help children learn to identify their feelings and understand that it is okay to experience a wide range of emotions.

Additionally, caregivers can encourage children to reflect on their feelings through activities such as journalism, drawing, or using emotion cards. These activities provide children with opportunities to express their emotions creatively and reinforce the idea that it is important to acknowledge and explore their feelings. For example, a caregiver might prompt a child to draw a picture that represents how they feel about a particular event, allowing the child to process their emotions in a non-verbal way.

Self-regulation, another critical component of emotional intelligence, involves managing one's emotions and behaviors in response to different situations. This skill enables children to cope with frustration, control impulses, and make thoughtful decisions rather than reacting emotionally. Teaching self-regulation begins with helping children develop coping strategies that they can use when they are feeling overwhelmed.

Caregivers can model self-regulation by demonstrating how to manage their own emotions during challenging situations. For instance, if a parent feels frustrated while cooking, they might say, "I'm feeling a bit stressed right now, so I'm going to take a deep breath and count to ten before I continue." This shows the child that it is possible to pause and regain composure before reacting. Additionally, caregivers can teach children specific self-regulation techniques, such as deep breathing, counting, or taking a break when they are feeling upset or angry.

Creating a calm-down space at home can also help children learn to self-regulate. This designated area, filled with calming items such as books, stress balls, or art supplies, provides a safe space where children can retreat when they need to manage their emotions. Caregivers can encourage children to use this space as a way to practice self-regulation, allowing them to develop a sense of ownership over their emotional well-being.

Social awareness is another crucial aspect of emotional intelligence that involves the ability to understand and empathize with the feelings and perspectives of others. Teaching social awareness begins with modeling empathy in everyday interactions. Caregivers can demonstrate empathetic behavior by actively listening to their children and validating their feelings. For example, if a child expresses frustration about a friend being mean, a caregiver might respond, "It sounds like that really hurt your feelings. It's tough when friends don't treat us kindly." This helps children learn that their feelings are valid and encourages them to consider how others might feel in similar situations.

Role-playing can also be an effective method for developing social awareness. Caregivers can create scenarios where children practice recognizing and responding to different emotions in others. For instance, a caregiver might act out a situation where one child is upset and the other is trying to comfort them. Afterward, the caregiver can ask questions such as, "How do you think that child felt? What could you say to help them feel better?" This type of practice reinforces the importance of empathy and helps children develop their social skills.

Building relationship management skills is the final component of emotional intelligence. Relationship management involves the ability to communicate effectively, resolve conflicts, and maintain healthy relationships. Children with strong relationship management skills are more likely to develop positive social connections and navigate conflicts in a constructive manner.

To foster relationship management skills, caregivers can teach children effective communication strategies. This includes using "I" statements to express feelings, actively listening to others, and negotiating solutions during disagreements. For example, when two siblings argue over a toy, a caregiver might guide them by saying, "Instead of yelling at each other, try using 'I' statements. One of you can say, 'I feel upset when I can't play with the toy' to express your feelings without blaming the other."

Encouraging teamwork through cooperative activities is another effective way to develop relationship management skills. Engaging in group projects, sports, or collaborative games helps children learn to work together, share responsibilities, and navigate challenges as a team. Caregivers can reinforce the importance of collaboration by discussing the skills they used to succeed, such as communication, compromise, and support.

It is also essential for children to learn how to handle conflicts constructively. Caregivers can teach conflict resolution strategies by guiding children through the process of resolving disagreements. This involves helping them identify the problem, express their feelings, and brainstorm potential solutions. For example, caregivers might say, "Let's take a moment to figure out what went wrong. Can you each explain how you feel? Then, we can come up with a solution together."

Practicing conflict resolution skills in real-life situations is an important step in reinforcing these lessons. Caregivers can provide support and guidance when conflicts arise, allowing children to practice their skills while also ensuring that they feel safe and supported. Celebrating successful conflict resolution moments reinforces the idea that disagreements can lead to positive outcomes when handled constructively.

Another effective way to build emotional intelligence is through storytelling and literature. Books and stories often explore complex emotions and social dynamics, making them excellent tools for teaching empathy and understanding. Caregivers can read stories with their children and discuss the characters' feelings, motivations, and actions. Questions like, "How do you think the character felt when that happened?" or "What could the character have done differently?" encourage children to think critically about emotions and social interactions.

Mindfulness practices can also contribute significantly to building emotional intelligence. Mindfulness helps children develop greater self-awareness and self-regulation by encouraging them to pay attention to their thoughts and feelings in the present moment. Mindfulness techniques can include deep breathing exercises, guided imagery, or simple meditation practices. For example, caregivers can guide their children through a short breathing exercise, encouraging them to focus on their breath and observe how they feel physically and emotionally. By incorporating mindfulness into daily routines, caregivers can help children cultivate emotional awareness and enhance their ability to manage stress and emotions.

Community involvement and social engagement can further enrich children's emotional intelligence. Participating in group activities, volunteering, or engaging in community service provides children with opportunities to connect with others, understand diverse perspectives, and develop empathy. These experiences not only help children build relationships but also foster a sense of belonging and purpose.

As children grow older, fostering emotional intelligence becomes increasingly important as they navigate the challenges of adolescence and adulthood. The skills learned in childhood provide a foundation for managing relationships, handling stress, and pursuing personal goals. Encouraging open discussions about emotions and relationships as children transition into their teenage years helps them refine their emotional intelligence and develop a deeper understanding of themselves and others.

Caregivers should continue to model emotional intelligence as children grow. Demonstrating self-regulation, effective communication, and empathy in their own interactions reinforces these skills and shows children that emotional intelligence is a lifelong journey. Engaging in open conversations about emotions, conflict resolution, and social dynamics creates an environment where children feel safe to express themselves and explore their feelings.

As children enter school and begin to interact more with their peers, it's essential to remain engaged in their emotional development. Caregivers should stay attuned to their child's social experiences, offering guidance and support as needed. This involvement allows caregivers to identify any challenges their child may be facing in developing emotional intelligence and provides opportunities for timely intervention and support.

In summary, building emotional intelligence is a vital long-term strategy for nurturing healthy, resilient children. By focusing on the key components of self-awareness, self-regulation, social awareness, and relationship management, caregivers and educators can provide children with the tools they need to navigate their emotions and relationships effectively. Through modeling, practice, and engagement, caregivers can help children develop strong emotional intelligence that will serve them well throughout their lives. As children learn to understand their own emotions and empathize with others, they become better equipped to face life's challenges, build meaningful connections, and thrive both personally and socially.

Creating a Positive Home Environment

Creating a positive home environment is essential for nurturing a child's emotional, social, and cognitive development. A home that promotes positivity, safety, and emotional well-being can significantly influence a child's behavior, self-esteem, and overall happiness. The foundation of a positive home environment lies in the relationships between family members, the structure and routine of daily life, and the physical space that surrounds the family. Each of these elements plays a crucial role in shaping the atmosphere of the home and contributes to the child's sense of security, belonging, and support.

At the heart of a positive home environment is the emotional climate created by the caregivers. Relationships characterized by love, respect, and open communication foster a sense of safety and trust. Children need to know they are loved and valued, which can be communicated through words, actions, and attentive behavior. Regular expressions of affection, such as hugs, compliments, and words of encouragement, reinforce the child's self-worth and help build a strong emotional connection between caregivers and children.

Open communication is also vital in establishing a positive home environment. Encouraging children to express their thoughts, feelings, and concerns creates a culture of trust and respect. Caregivers should model effective communication skills by actively listening to their children, validating their feelings, and responding thoughtfully. This two-way communication not only helps children feel heard and understood but also teaches them how to express themselves in a constructive manner. For example, asking open-ended questions like, "How was your day?" or "What made you feel happy today?" invites children to share their experiences and fosters deeper conversations.

Creating family traditions and rituals can also enhance the emotional climate of the home. Regular family activities, such as family dinners, game nights, or weekend outings, provide opportunities for bonding and strengthen relationships. These shared experiences create lasting memories and a sense of belonging, which is especially important for children as they develop their identity and social skills. Family rituals can also offer comfort and stability, particularly during times of change or stress, helping children feel grounded and connected to their family.

Another crucial aspect of a positive home environment is the structure and routine established by caregivers. Children thrive on routine, as it provides a sense of predictability and security in their daily lives. Having consistent schedules for meals, homework, chores, and bedtime helps children know what to expect and reduces anxiety. For example, a structured evening routine might include dinner, followed by time for reading or quiet play, and then a consistent bedtime. This routine not only helps children feel secure but also teaches them important life skills, such as time management and responsibility.

Flexibility is also important within the structure of routines. While consistency provides stability, it's essential for caregivers to remain adaptable to accommodate the child's needs and preferences. Life is full of unexpected changes, and teaching children how to navigate these changes helps them develop resilience and adaptability. For example, if a planned family outing is disrupted by bad weather, caregivers can encourage children to find alternative activities that can be enjoyed indoors, reinforcing the idea that flexibility is a valuable life skill.

A positive home environment should also prioritize emotional well-being and mental health. This involves creating a space where children feel safe to express their emotions without fear of judgment or reprimand. Caregivers should validate children's feelings and provide support during difficult moments. For example, if a child is upset after a challenging day at school, a caregiver might say, "It's okay to feel sad about what happened. Do you want to talk about it?" This approach teaches children that it is normal to experience a range of emotions and that they can seek support when needed.

In addition to emotional support, caregivers can foster mental well-being by promoting positive coping strategies. Teaching children healthy ways to manage stress and emotions equips them with the tools they need to navigate challenges throughout their lives. This might include introducing relaxation techniques, such as deep breathing exercises, mindfulness practices, or physical activities like yoga or sports. By encouraging these positive coping mechanisms, caregivers help children learn to regulate their emotions and manage stress in a healthy way.

Creating a positive physical environment is equally important in nurturing a child's development. A safe, organized, and stimulating home environment fosters exploration, creativity, and learning. Caregivers should ensure that the home is free from hazards and that children have access to age-appropriate toys and materials that encourage play and discovery. A well-organized space allows children to navigate their environment easily and encourages them to take responsibility for their belongings.

Additionally, caregivers should create designated areas within the home for different activities, such as a quiet reading nook, a creative arts and crafts area, or a space for active play. Having these distinct spaces allows children to engage in a variety of activities and promotes a sense of ownership over their environment. This organization also helps children learn to manage their time and responsibilities, as they can easily transition from one activity to another.

The aesthetics of the home can also contribute to a positive environment. A clean, inviting, and well-decorated space can uplift moods and create a sense of comfort. Personal touches, such as family photos, children's artwork, or plants, help create a warm and welcoming atmosphere. Caregivers should encourage children to contribute to the decoration of their space, fostering a sense of pride and ownership in their environment. For instance, allowing children to choose how to arrange their room or decorate a personal space with their favorite colors and designs can enhance their emotional connection to their surroundings.

Incorporating nature into the home environment can also have a positive impact on emotional well-being. Studies have shown that spending time outdoors and connecting with nature can reduce stress, improve mood, and enhance overall well-being. Caregivers can encourage outdoor play, gardening, or nature walks, allowing children to explore the natural world and develop a sense of wonder and appreciation for their environment. Creating a small indoor garden or bringing in houseplants can also help bring elements of nature into the home, contributing to a calming and nurturing atmosphere.

Technology can play a role in shaping the home environment, and caregivers should be mindful of its use. While technology can provide educational opportunities and connect families, it can also lead to over-stimulation and disconnection from real-life interactions. Establishing boundaries around screen time is essential for maintaining a healthy balance. Caregivers should model healthy technology habits by engaging in screen-free activities and prioritizing family time over digital distractions. For example, designating "device-free" family dinners or game nights encourages meaningful interactions and strengthens family bonds.

Another critical aspect of creating a positive home environment is fostering a growth mindset. Teaching children that mistakes and challenges are opportunities for learning helps them develop resilience and a love for learning. Caregivers can reinforce this mindset by praising effort rather than just outcomes. For example, instead of saying, "You got an A on your test; you're so smart," caregivers can say, "I'm proud of how hard you studied for that test. Your effort really paid off." This approach encourages children to embrace challenges and persist in the face of difficulties, knowing that effort and perseverance are valued.

Encouraging a culture of gratitude within the home can also contribute to a positive environment. Practicing gratitude helps children appreciate what they have and fosters a sense of contentment. Caregivers can incorporate gratitude practices into daily routines, such as sharing what each family member is thankful for at dinner or creating a gratitude jar where everyone can contribute notes of appreciation. This practice cultivates a positive outlook and strengthens family connections by focusing on the good in each other and the world around them.

Establishing family goals and values can further enhance the positive environment at home. Engaging children in discussions about what values are important to the family—such as kindness, respect, honesty, and hard work—helps them internalize these principles and apply them in their interactions with others. Creating family goals, such as volunteering together or working on a community project, fosters a sense of teamwork and shared purpose, reinforcing the idea that the family unit is a supportive and collaborative environment.

It's important to recognize that no family is perfect, and challenges will inevitably arise in any home environment. Conflict and disagreements are natural parts of family life, and teaching children how to navigate these challenges constructively is an important life skill. Caregivers should model healthy conflict resolution strategies, demonstrating how to communicate openly, listen actively, and find solutions together. For example, if a disagreement arises between siblings, caregivers can guide the children through a discussion where they express their feelings and work together to find a compromise.

Encouraging a sense of autonomy and independence in children is also essential for fostering a positive home environment. Children need opportunities to make choices and take on responsibilities, as this helps them build confidence and a sense of agency. Caregivers can provide age-appropriate tasks for children, such as helping with household chores, planning family activities, or making decisions about their own daily routines. By allowing children to take ownership of their responsibilities, caregivers help them develop essential life skills while also reinforcing their self-worth and competence.

Finally, caregivers should prioritize self-care and personal well-being. Creating a positive home environment begins with the emotional health of the adults in the home. Caregivers who practice self-care, seek support when needed, and manage their stress levels are better equipped to provide a nurturing environment for their children. Engaging in activities that bring joy and fulfillment, whether it's exercise, hobbies, or spending time with friends, helps caregivers maintain their well-being and create a more positive atmosphere at home.

In summary, creating a positive home environment involves nurturing relationships, establishing structure, promoting emotional well-being, and fostering a sense of belonging. By focusing on open communication, empathy, and positive reinforcement, caregivers can help children develop the emotional intelligence and resilience needed to navigate life's challenges. Additionally, creating a safe, organized, and stimulating physical environment supports exploration and creativity, while family traditions and rituals enhance connections and belonging. With patience, intention, and a commitment to fostering a positive atmosphere, caregivers can create a home that nurtures children's growth, development, and happiness.

Conclusion

Creating a comprehensive conclusion that encapsulates key strategies in parenting while emphasizing the importance of consistency is crucial for providing a clear pathway for parents seeking to enhance their effectiveness. Throughout the parenting journey, various strategies can be employed to foster healthy emotional and behavioral development in children. It is essential to recap these strategies as they form a cohesive framework that parents can implement in their daily lives.

One of the foundational strategies for effective parenting is the development of emotional intelligence in children. Building emotional intelligence involves teaching children to recognize, understand, and manage their emotions, as well as those of others. This can be achieved through open communication, modeling emotional regulation, and encouraging empathy. By engaging children in conversations about their feelings and those of their peers, parents can help them navigate their emotions and develop strong interpersonal skills. Practical methods, such as using storybooks that explore emotions or role-playing various scenarios, can provide children with valuable insights into understanding and managing emotions.

In addition to emotional intelligence, establishing clear and consistent routines is vital for creating a sense of stability and security in children. Routines help children feel more comfortable in their environment, as they know what to expect and can anticipate daily activities. By incorporating structured schedules for meals, homework, playtime, and bedtime, parents can foster a sense of predictability that supports the child's emotional well-being. Consistency in routines also allows children to develop important life skills, such as time management and responsibility.

Another critical strategy is the importance of positive reinforcement in shaping children's behavior. By focusing on encouraging desired behaviors rather than simply punishing undesirable ones, parents can promote a more positive atmosphere. Positive reinforcement can take many forms, including verbal praise, tangible rewards, or increased privileges. For example, parents can praise children when they display appropriate behaviors, such as sharing or completing tasks, reinforcing the idea that positive actions lead to positive outcomes. Celebrating small successes boosts a child's self-esteem and encourages them to continue making good choices.

Teaching effective communication skills is also essential for fostering healthy relationships and reducing conflict. Encouraging children to express their feelings and needs openly helps them develop the ability to communicate effectively in various situations. Parents can model active listening and use "I" statements to express their feelings without blaming or criticizing others. For instance, saying "I feel upset when you don't help with chores" promotes constructive dialogue, while emphasizing that feelings are valid. These skills not only benefit the child's interactions at home but also equip them for successful social relationships outside the family.

Conflict resolution skills are another critical area to focus on in parenting. Children must learn how to handle disagreements and resolve conflicts constructively. Teaching them to approach conflicts with empathy and understanding, and to seek mutually beneficial solutions, is crucial for their social development. Role-playing different scenarios and guiding children through the process of finding solutions can empower them to navigate disputes effectively. When conflicts arise, parents should act as facilitators, helping children articulate their feelings and negotiate solutions rather than merely intervening to resolve the issue themselves.

CONCLUSION

Creating a positive home environment is a multifaceted strategy that encompasses all of the previously mentioned elements. A nurturing environment promotes emotional security, open communication, and healthy relationships. This includes ensuring that the home is a safe and organized space, where children feel valued and supported. Establishing family rituals, such as regular family meals or game nights, fosters connection and creates lasting memories. Furthermore, being attuned to children's emotional needs and recognizing their unique personalities helps caregivers tailor their approach, ensuring that each child feels understood and loved.

Encouraging resilience in children is also a vital aspect of effective parenting. Children need to learn how to cope with setbacks, challenges, and disappointments as part of their growth and development. Fostering a growth mindset—the belief that abilities and intelligence can be developed through effort and persistence—can empower children to approach challenges with confidence. When children encounter difficulties, parents should emphasize effort and the learning process rather than solely focusing on outcomes. Phrases like "I'm proud of how hard you tried" can reinforce the value of perseverance and encourage children to keep pushing forward despite obstacles.

Parental involvement in education is another essential strategy for supporting a child's development. Actively participating in a child's education—through attending parent-teacher conferences, helping with homework, and engaging in school activities—demonstrates the importance of education and fosters a love of learning. When children see their parents valuing education, they are more likely to take it seriously themselves. Additionally, collaborating with teachers to create an environment that supports the child's learning needs helps ensure a holistic approach to education.

Fostering independence is also key to effective parenting. While it's essential to provide guidance and support, children should also have opportunities to make choices and take on responsibilities appropriate for their age. Encouraging children to help with household chores, manage their own schedules, and make decisions fosters a sense of agency and self-reliance. Parents can guide them through this process, allowing them to learn from their mistakes and celebrate their successes. Building independence prepares children for the challenges of adulthood and helps them develop confidence in their abilities.

In addition to these strategies, it's vital for parents to prioritize their well-being and practice self-care. Parenting can be challenging, and caregivers must take care of their physical, emotional, and mental health to be effective role models. When parents are healthy and balanced, they are better equipped to support their children through life's ups and downs. Engaging in self-care activities—whether it's exercise, hobbies, or spending time with friends—ensures that caregivers can recharge and remain present and attentive to their children's needs.

Lastly, the importance of building a strong support network cannot be understated. Parenting can be isolating at times, and having a network of friends, family, or community resources provides invaluable support. Whether it's sharing experiences with other parents, seeking advice from trusted mentors, or participating in parenting groups, these connections can help caregivers feel less alone in their journey. Building relationships with others who understand the challenges of parenting fosters a sense of community and provides opportunities for collaboration and shared learning.

In summary, the strategies for creating a positive home environment and promoting emotional intelligence in children are interconnected and mutually reinforcing. By focusing on open communication, establishing routines, using positive reinforcement, teaching conflict resolution, and fostering resilience, parents can provide children with the tools they need to thrive. Each strategy contributes to a nurturing atmosphere that prioritizes emotional well-being and personal growth. Consistent parenting, characterized by patience, empathy, and understanding, is essential for implementing these strategies effectively.

CONCLUSION

A consistent approach to parenting involves applying these strategies with regularity and intention. Children thrive when they know what to expect and when their caregivers respond to their needs in predictable ways. Consistency helps children feel secure and reinforces their understanding of acceptable behaviors and emotional expression. As children grow and develop, their needs may change, and caregivers must remain adaptable while maintaining the core values and principles that guide their parenting.

The journey of parenting is not without its challenges, but by embracing these strategies and committing to consistent parenting, caregivers can create a positive environment that fosters their children's emotional intelligence, resilience, and overall well-being. Building a foundation of emotional awareness, healthy communication, and mutual respect sets the stage for children to develop into confident, empathetic individuals who are well-equipped to navigate the complexities of life.

www.ingramcontent.com/pod-product-compliance
Lightning Source LLC
Chambersburg PA
CBHW050303230526
45471CB00005B/1999